European Futures

Scenarios are by definition imaginary. If the authors have shown too much or too little imagination, they alone are responsible. Neither their views nor their perceptions must be taken to be those of the European Commission.

European Futures

Five Possible Scenarios for 2010

Gilles Bertrand, Anna Michalski and Lucio R. Pench
Forward Studies Unit, European Commission

Edward Elgar
Cheltenham, UK • Northampton MA, USA

Published by
Edward Elgar Publishing Limited
Glensanda House
Montpellier Parade
Cheltenham
Glos GL50 1UA
UK

Edward Elgar Publishing, Inc.
136 West Street
Suite 202
Northampton
Massachusetts 01060
USA

A catalogue record for this book
is available from the British Library

Library of Congress Cataloguing in Publication Data

Bertrand, Gilles, 1972–
    European futures : five possible scenarios for 2010 / Gilles Bertrand, Anna
Michalski, and Lucio Pench.
    1. Europe—Forecasting.   I. Michalski, Anna.   II. Pench, Lucio R., 1957–
III. Title.

HN373 B47 2000
303.494—dc21   00–037607

ISBN 1 84064 450 8
Printed and bound in Great Britain by MPG Books Ltd, Bodmin, Cornwall

Contents

Acknowledgements

From its very beginning this project was intended as a team effort (one could say a collective learning exercise), so acknowledgements are owed to a large number of people. The choice was made to mention on the cover page only the three persons who were involved in it from beginning to end and undertook the actual writing of the *Scenarios* – but we should also pay tribute to Paul Gerd Loeser for the many discussions that led to the initial idea; to Agne Pantelouri and Marjorie Jouen who were major contributors to the first stage (Marjorie, some say your spirit still lingers across the pages!); and to Notis Lebessis who helped us to sharpen our reflection while we were battling with the writing.

The collective nature of the exercise is illustrated by the number and the diversity of colleagues from the Commission who were involved in the working groups. Their names are listed at the end of this publication. We owe a special mention to the *happy few* who took part in the elaboration of the global scenarios: Michel Biart, Paraskevas Caracostas, Jean-François Drevet, David Hudson, Ana Melich, John Norman Pyres, Adrian Taylor, Axel Walldén and Francis Woehrling. Some other colleagues gave us useful advice at the right time: Knut Kuebler on energy, Gustavo Fahrenkrog and other IPTS colleagues on science and technology, René Leray on defence matters and Mark Gray on institutional issues. Mark also gave his friendly help with the English language editing.

Many thanks as well to Luc Wagner for the computer tool, to Bénédicte Carémier for managing the contacts with the publishers, to Abdellah Arabate, Ann Grossi and Sylvie Barès for the final formatting – and of course to Pamela Cranston for supporting us in the administration of the project, doubting that the *Scenarios* would ever be finished ... and being the great and reliable colleague she is.

We are also grateful to Anne Buckingham, Susan Maclure, Jonathan Stockwell from the Translation Department for their remarkable and enthusiastic work, to all the people across Europe who helped us to organize the test presentations and to all the trainees who gave a helping hand at some stage: Tom Hampson, Stefan Ilcus, Yke de Jong, Liselotte Lyngsø, Célina Ramjoué, Luc Reuter, Jonas Tallberg, Rupert Weinmann, to name but a few.

The authors are also indebted to the support given to the project by President Santer and his Cabinet.

Finally, our warmest thanks to our former Director Jérôme Vignon for pushing the project forward when not everyone believed in it – and to his successor Jean-Claude Thébault for his permanent support, advice and confidence in our work.

Gilles Bertrand, Anna Michalski, Lucio R. Pench

Introduction

Every epoch is an epoch of transition.
We know only one thing about the future
or, rather, the futures:
it will not look like the present.

Jorge Luis Borges

The notion that Europe at the start of the third millennium is facing many challenges has gained widespread credence. The fact that our societies along with their values and traditions are changing rapidly is also commonly accepted. Daily, the threats and opportunities stemming from new technologies are the subject of numerous public debates. Our political leaders incessantly reiterate that we must find new ways to deal with the complexity of our contemporary world. Very seldom, however, are concrete examples presented in order to give people the opportunity to form an idea of how the future of Europe might look. Even more rarely are coherent and contrasted illustrations given of how Europe may evolve in the future as the result of actions and decisions that are taken today.

Aware of this lacuna, the Forward Studies Unit of the European Commission launched at the beginning of 1997 a project, *Scenarios Europe 2010*, with the objective of producing a set of coherent and thought-provoking images of the future of Europe. It is the hope that by studying these scenarios the reader will be encouraged to reflect both on the changes that are taking place in the world and on the options that lie ahead.

Many elements contribute to the process of societal change. The transition from the agrarian and industrial societies to the information society has not only prompted new modes of living and a different, less hierarchical organization for society, but has also generated new values and aspirations for individuals. Scientific know-how has become so advanced as to allow humans to influence the cause of events on a large scale, and the possibilities of communicating and travelling have rendered the world a subjectively smaller place. In this world of constant mutation, individual citizens are looking for answers to complex questions and to new frames of reference against which the world can be understood.

In contemporary society, it is recognized that public policies and the way they are conducted are becoming increasingly complex. This postulates that efficient formulation and application of policies is dependent on the ability of organizations to take in a multitude of facts, to interpret these facts from a variety of angles and to update policies continuously in order to reflect the changes in the context for which they were initially aimed. In this context of uncertainty, a better and more versatile understanding of the future and the deep trends influencing its evolution can assist policy-makers in identifying future needs and developing appropriate policy initiatives to meet them. For European citizens to participate actively in the shaping of Europe's future, it is important for them to acquire a broader insight into the interplay between driving trends, structural elements, ideologies and policy outcomes.

Illustrating the future by means of scenarios is a way to overcome human beings' innate resistance to change. Scenarios can open mental horizons that allow the individual to accept and understand change, and so be able to shape the world. Scenarios may help in seizing new opportunities in advance as well as avoiding the undesirable effects of misconceived actions. The principal aim of *Scenarios Europe 2010* was therefore twofold: to stimulate debate inside and outside the Commission on the future of European integration; and to develop a tool to put the Union's policies and strategies into perspective and contribute to their improvement.

The project *Scenarios Europe 2010* relied on the expertise of civil servants of the European Commission. Through a process of structured brainstorming and step-by-step synthesis (see Chapter 8 'How We Built the Scenarios'), the background knowledge and the emerging ideas of the participants were drawn together into a global project. Responsibility for organizing the process and for the actual writing of the scenarios fell entirely on the Forward Studies Unit, and particularly on the authors of the present publication. The entire exercise, which took about two years, was also aimed at fostering a 'future culture' inside the Commission. As officials from different departments are encouraged to know more about the future limits and opportunities in policy areas other than their own, it should be possible for a more integrated and forward-looking approach to policy-making to emerge.

The scenarios are entirely qualitative in nature. They present a number of plausible, internally coherent illustrations of the future of Europe to which no probability is attached. Scenarios are not, and cannot be, either a projection of the future, or a prediction of the likelihood of a certain outcome. Deliberately, none of the scenarios is entirely rosy and none is entirely dark. Each scenario contains positive and negative aspects that allow for a composite, even contrasted, picture of the future – like, indeed, our contemporary world. The exercise was designed not to make value judgements, since 'good' or 'bad', put in a specific context, mean different things to different people. There was also an attempt not to make the scenarios too complex in the sense that each scenario should have a character of its own with easily recognizable features.

For the same reason it was decided that a trend scenario would not be developed, not because a continuation of present trends is unlikely, but rather because, for the purpose of intellectual stimulus, other alternative scenarios are more interesting and their consequences more compelling. Finally, a narrative style was chosen in order to facilitate the reading and in the hope of making the reader 'feel' the implications of different future outcomes.

The qualitative nature of the scenarios and the choice of a narrative style are of course no excuse for dispensing with a rigorous review of the factors that are bound to influence the future of Europe. Besides the expertise contributed by the participants to the scenario-building exercise, the Forward Studies Unit engaged in an analysis of a number of deep-lying trends affecting Europe that are broadly speaking 'set' within the time horizon of 2010. The illustration of the trends is a necessary complement to the scenarios in order to give the reader a multi-faceted and more complete picture of the future. For this reason they are included in the present publication (see Chapter 6 'What We Know About the Future').

At the beginning of the twenty-first century, many commentators have underlined the importance of a wide public debate on the future of Europe. These scenarios are intended to contribute to such a debate by forming the background for a meaningful discussion and by offering the participants the possibility to acquire a common language.

When studying the scenarios, it is up to the readers to assess, on the basis of their experience, beliefs and expectations, which combination of them best corresponds to their idea of Europe in 2010.

1. Scenario no. 1: Triumphant Markets

In his annual state-of-the-world speech to the United Nations General Assembly, the American President recently described the twenty-first century as a 'triumph of trade over war'. This optimistic description fairly accurately summarizes the state of mind in the West at the start of the second decade of the twenty-first century. The industrialized countries have returned to full employment. World trade continues to grow in a spectacular fashion. Helped by technological innovation, productivity has revived, even in the sectors where traditionally it tended to stagnate. Above all, the economic ideas of the developed countries are dominating everywhere: most states in the world, apart from a few exceptions, have espoused the principles of free trade, and have used the last 15 years to disengage from economic life. Europe has followed suit, breaking with sometimes century-old traditions of extravagant social expenditure and strong public intervention. Thanks to the thorough reforms carried out since 2005 and the stability of the euro, it has in the space of a few years gone from wobbly competitiveness to a performance comparable to that of the United States. As for the social cataclysm predicted by some, it has not (yet?) happened. Inequality and exclusion have increased, but remain at tolerable levels, to judge by the absence of mass popular protest.

The first signs that the European social market economy was running out of steam appeared fairly far back in the twentieth century, but it has taken more than a generation for Europe to fully draw the consequences. The creation of the European Single Market, the privatization of public enterprises and the gradual suppression of state aid were achieved without any major blips from the 1980s onwards. However, the reduction in social protection systems was more difficult, even though they had clearly reached a point of no return: on the one hand, a globalized economy, fluid, competitive, on a permanent quest for flexibility; on the other, disorganized *welfare states* made untenable by the ageing of the population – and letting increasing numbers slip through the net into social exclusion. This analysis was broadly shared at the end of the last century, but the erratic largesse of the system meant there was something in it for most Europeans, and the politicians still wanted to believe in a third way.

It was the development of the world economy that swept away Europe's uncertainties. In 2002–2003, it became clear that American productivity had hit a phase of growth that was both sustainable and faster than anywhere else in the industrialized world. The United States was living the premise of the long-heralded *Third Industrial Revolution*, and modernization was extended even to supposedly untouchable sectors such as education, health and social assistance. This explosion seemed to be intrinsically linked to the way American society was organized and to the values it reflected: by favouring entrepreneurship and quick profits, by making individuals responsible for their education and for coping with life's uncertainties, American society achieved an unparalleled degree of fluidity which enabled it to take full advantage of the potential of the new information technologies. Confronted with this relatively indisputable fact, no region in the world was able to come up with a credible alternative: neither Asia, which based its economic revival on the gradual adoption of an Anglo-Saxon model of capitalism, nor Europe, which was too concerned with cobbling together solutions for constantly soaring social expenditure. There were still some orators who extolled Asian values or the European social model, but their words remained sadly divorced from reality.

Once again, the *old continent*'s traditional fear of decline raised its head: with the United States surging ahead, Europe did not appear to have any choice other than to take up the *American challenge* – or to disengage from the dynamism of the world economy. From that moment, the politicians started to appropriate the values of free enterprise and denounce the aberrations of the welfare state. Benefit fraudsters, malingerers, public sector employees, scroungers of all kinds were pilloried like so many *shirkers* unfairly living off taxpayers' money. Against a background of generalized distrust of the state, a consensus emerged around both individualist and free-market values, sustained by the will to 'free individuals from constraints', which meant refusing assistance, respecting wealth and social success, and believing in the ability of competition to reabsorb abuses of the system. At the same time, the European public became more tolerant of the perverse effects of these values, particularly the growth in income inequality, and the ever-increasing importance of money in everyday life. The political turnaround came between 2003 and 2005: massively rejecting the moribund unions and a seriously ailing social democracy, European voters handed over the reins of their countries to a new generation of politicians, who buckled down to dismantling the welfare state, despite enormous resistance.

The first step was to give Europeans back 'a job at any price'. With the reduction in unemployment benefit and the abolition of recruitment and wage restrictions, European businesses now have a flexible workforce and adjustable wage costs: low for non-qualified tasks, and very high for top-calibre employees whose earnings have to be in line with those elsewhere in the world. This growing dichotomy has stimulated the whole economy, from high-tech industries to personal services, which wage costs had previously prevented from growing in spite of strong potential demand. Unemployment, previously presented as an inescapable evil, has dropped massively, and certain regions of the continent are even facing chronic labour shortages (in spite of the large influx of migrants, often from the poorest Member States). The only blot on the landscape is that the considerable increase in low-skilled, insecure and poorly paid jobs has led to the emergence of a *working poor* class.

At the same time, over the last five years governments have made substantial reductions in public expenditure by completing privatizations, reducing the number of civil servants (made possible by abolishing job security), privatizing sickness insurance, reducing pension systems and imposing strict means testing for the award of social security benefits. The public sector has also seen its powers decline: in most EU countries, the state now confines itself to maintaining public order and the judicial system, and does not intervene in other areas unless no one else is prepared to do so. Its administrative tasks are largely subcontracted out to private enterprise, and cost has become the main criterion for the evaluation of public policies. As a whole, this *value for money* philosophy has made state employees more responsible and more efficient (at least according to measurable, short-term criteria). However, it leaves undeveloped whole sectors in which public action would be useful in the long term, though not measurable in strictly financial terms. For example, there are many major infrastructure projects that remain on hold for lack of public funds, perpetuating the supremacy of road freight – which is however less sustainable and more polluting than other forms of transport. In the same vein, some economists consider that the quality of the continent's infrastructure is already starting to decline.

Overall, however, the European economies have emerged from the streamlining process more competitive and more flexible. Whether in growth, consumption or employment, the macroeconomic indicators have mainly returned to good health. The experts reckon that inflation will not reappear in Europe for the foreseeable future: not just because the European stability pact is working well, but, more importantly, because the classic inflationary spiral (wages/prices) is hard to imagine in such deregulated goods and labour markets. The whole economy has been reorganized in a more fluid manner, in step with technological innovation. Small businesses have multiplied, and they are often very open to the international environment, developing in high-added-value sectors and generally employing highly qualified staff. Some of them have even, after years of unrestrained growth, become real multi-nationals, joining the American 'gazelles' on the list of economic success stories.

Of course Europe is not the only one to have been swept along by the current of free trade. There is now a worldwide consensus in favour of the market economy, even if most countries in the world submit to rather than shape the process. NAFTA, the EU, ASEAN and, to a lesser degree, Japan, are emerging as indefatigable advocates of free trade: they share the desire to strengthen the WTO's role, and the last few years have laid the foundation for an ambitious co-operation between America, Europe and Asia on economic and trade questions, particularly dispute settlement. While not exhibiting the same enthusiasm, Russia and China are sustained by quite good economic results, and they are (for now) in step with the world trend. Even if it is tempting to make China an exception, Beijing must now come to terms with the rise of the coastal regions, which are more prosperous and completely in favour of opening up to the outside world. As for Russia, it is adopting an increasingly predictable and open attitude to its neighbours in return for being reintegrated into the world economic game. Finally, with varying degrees of resistance, most developing countries have initiated a process of deregulation and reform. Only a minority remain outside the world current: some quasi-autarkic states, a dozen or so micro-potentates with vast natural resources, and several regional powers opposing the *Westernization* of the world for ideological or religious reasons.

All the evidence suggests that the momentum of the free market should become even more marked in the years to come: with the increasing importance of intangible goods, it is becoming almost impossible to buck the trend. Several proposals are circulating which would have looked like incoherent daydreams only a few years ago. For example, since their economic approaches are broadly convergent, the three great monetary powers are planning to co-ordinate their budgetary policies more closely and limit the fluctuations between the yen, the euro and the dollar. This project has a good chance of being welcomed by the rest of the world, which has had enough of what has sometimes been called the monetary unilateralism of Europe and the United States. Seizing the dynamism of the moment and the goodwill of the main world players, Washington and Brussels have also proposed the launch of a *Planet Round*, in other words new trade negotiations, to create a global free-trade area by 2025.

Of course, deregulation is only one element in the virtuous circle behind the vigour of the world economy. In fact, we are witnessing the conjunction of several favourable factors. First of all, technological development is faster than ever before. Almost everywhere in the world, the combination of satellites and fibre optics offers infinite possibilities for communication and access to information at low cost, and the experts are predicting imminent breakthroughs in other areas: biotechnologies, artificial intelligence, energy, etc. The continual increase in the number of consumers also explains the healthy state of the world economy: according to the most recent estimates, one billion human beings now enjoy a standard of living and consumption habits comparable to Western countries. However, apart from a few improvements (in health care for example), the remaining 6 billion have stagnated at the same level of destitution as 20 or 30 years ago. Social inequalities are greater than ever in developing countries, including those undergoing rapid economic development.

The wind of reform and the neo-liberal trend have also brought with them thoroughgoing reforms of the structures and powers of the European Union. The Union's most expensive policies were attacked from all sides in the first opening years of the century. The year 2005 was a watershed: the heads of state, for the most part newly elected, demanded a renegotiation of the Community budget. The eve of the first enlargement of the Union to Central and Eastern Europe was the last opportunity to reduce Community expenditure before new members who set greater store by financial solidarity joined, so the Member States agreed on a radical reform of the agricultural policy: reduction of subsidies, renationalisation of management (subject to common rules being laid down) and the gradual alignment of European prices with world markets. It was also planned to gradually reduce the funds allocated to regional policy. The leader of the Dutch conservative party welcomed the results of the European Council with an allusion to the well-known fable of La Fontaine: 'it was time that the ants stopped feeding the grasshoppers'.

Apart from these cosmetic changes to the budget, the Member States also chose to postpone plans for European political integration. It must be said that enlargement to the East is the only project on which all the Member States agree: the Single Market is complete, and the other projects are bones of continual contention. Construction of an area of internal security is officially a priority for the Union, but it has been slowed down by the unanimity rule. As regards foreign policy, the vast majority of the Member States prefer to see the Union concentrate on economic questions: the Europeans rely on NATO for military issues, and they have persuaded their American partners to mould the Atlantic Alliance into a structure to prevent conflicts in areas bordering the EU. The increasing involvement of Russia has some observers speaking of an impending 'OSCEization' of NATO. (For the rest, in the absence of any risk of major conflict, governments all over the world are concentrating on economic questions: even the Pentagon considers that the United States' world supremacy stems above all from their technological lead.) The other political projects that the EU was nurturing at the end of the last century, such as a social Europe or the ideal of sustainable development, are no longer on the agenda, and the Member States whose competitiveness has remained the most fragile, particularly the Central and Eastern European states, refuse the new constraints which any increase in Union activity in these areas would bring in their wake. This lack of a shared political project is, of course, reflected in the institutions: the European authorities remain unchallenged in the economic and commercial fields (the European Commission for competition and state aid and the European Central Bank for monetary policy), but all attempts over the last 15 years to make the institutional system more effective and more efficient have ended in failure. The last attempt, at Karlsruhe in 2007, led only to minor improvements, and neither the Member States nor the Commission now dare to call for a new intergovernmental conference.

In the absence of other ambitions, it is therefore the enlargement of the Single Market (and the euro zone) which has become the absolute priority in Brussels, and accessions and applications are coming thick and fast. Reassured by the abandonment of the political project, Switzerland, Iceland and Norway jointly reapplied and joined the Union in 2004. The countries of Central and Eastern Europe, Cyprus and Malta all joined between 2005 and 2008. As for Turkey, it intends to conclude the negotiations begun in 2007 within four years, and should soon become the 31st member of the Union. Several new candidates with mainly economic motives are also crowding at the gate, such as Ukraine, the Balkan countries, and also Israel, Lebanon and Morocco. It is not certain that the Union will decide to expand beyond the European continent, but it has already announced its ambition to create a customs union with Russia and the other countries of the former USSR, and the Euro-Mediterranean free-trade zone has now been set up. Some people are already dreaming of a huge market stretching 'from the Sahara to Siberia', but they are thinking more of a free-trade area than a Single Market covered by all the Community policies. It is notable that none of them is proposing to facilitate the movement of people within this immense emerging economic space, which has led some sceptics to comment that the Europeans are openly constructing a world where goods are freer than people.

Behind the dream of a frontier-free economy, however, more dangerous realities are looming. First of all, the risks in terms of non-military security (*soft security*) are proliferating. International crime is undoubtedly the most serious: criminal organizations of all kinds are making the most of the new fluidity of world trade, and their impunity is guaranteed in practice by the ineffectiveness of badly equipped police systems, still organized at national levels. Trafficking in arms, drugs and human beings is constantly on the increase, and Europe is particularly vulnerable to the black market in illegal immigrants, via southern and Eastern Europe. The threat of terrorism has also remained constant, and the developed countries, particularly the United States, are unquestionably the prime targets. In general, criminal networks (whatever their aim) are now more adaptable and complex than ever. The routes along which information or trafficked products travel are constantly changing, and the mafias rarely use the same middleman twice. Furthermore, economic prosperity has left enough people by the wayside for there to be no shortage of recruits: petty criminals in troubled cities and hard-up Third World guerrillas willingly agree to act as one-off middlemen for organized crime. International police co-operation remains notoriously inadequate to deal with these new-style organizations (even in Europe, in spite of belated attempts to strengthen Europol).

The speed of economic development is also imposing ever more intolerable constraints on the planet's ecosystem. The 1990s showed the beginnings of an international awareness about the environment, but it was never strong enough to override more immediate considerations. The recent United Nations summits on natural resources have all been fiascos: television viewers throughout the world have got used to seeing rich countries and developing countries blame each other for the ecological disaster, and use global competition as an excuse for putting off urgent decisions. Actually, the ecological situation is improving in relative terms in the rich countries, but worsening everywhere else. While ever greater numbers of people are acquiring the consumption habits of the developed countries, infrastructure and waste-processing systems are failing to keep pace: the gigantic traffic jams in Africa's sprawling cities, the mass of plastic detritus swept along by most of the great Asian rivers, the rapid destruction of fish reserves and of tropical rain forests all show, in their different ways, that the human race is still far from achieving a way of developing sustainably, and has even moved in the opposite direction. The developed countries are showing themselves to be exceptionally penny-pinching and blind in the face of this danger. The European Union is being accused by its Central and Eastern European members and its Mediterranean neighbours of deliberately ignoring the scale of financial need, while the continent's stability is increasingly threatened by shortages of drinking water in North Africa, the dying Mediterranean and the many types of industrial and agricultural pollution further north.

Increasing inequality is another worrying spin-off in the current system. First of all, certain countries look well and truly as though they have been *left on the world's scrap heap*, with the greater part of their population still stagnating below the absolute poverty line. Worse still, social and regional imbalances are actually growing within states, whatever their level of economic advancement. In the developing countries, the gulf is increasing between cities and the countryside, creating an exodus of rural people from the countryside into towns where health, law and order, and the environment are on the verge of collapse. In the developed countries, the outermost regions have to make do with the crumbs of economic growth, while the quality of their infrastructure and public services steadily declines. In Europe, certain areas have become depopulated and are now no more than havens of tranquillity for exhausted city-dwellers. At the other end of the spectrum, at the heart of the information society, the most innovative cities and regions are steaming ahead. Between the two extremes, most regions are trying to hitch themselves to one or two of these economic champions, but at the cost of increasing dependence. These *hinterland* situations are politically problematical: for example, certain Central European countries jibe at the idea of being relegated to the status of satellites of the richest regions of Germany or the Baltic.

The change in European values also gives cause for concern. European societies are without a doubt more fragmented than ever. Individualism and relativism are dominant, leading the continent towards worrying collective choices (by default). Consumerism and the desire for permanent innovation orchestrated by advertising are overriding the big ideas, and the Europeans are now limiting their desire for solidarity to their immediate entourage, particularly their family. Generally, the public distrusts collective action, particularly by governments and public services. It is attracted more to associations and NGOs, but these only succeed in mobilizing it with short-lived publicity stunts. Finally, European cities are ensnared in the vicious circle of the security debate: distrust and inequalities fan the flames of urban crime and whip up racist tensions (a conflation now well established in political rhetoric), which in turn drive up the demand for security and ever-more extreme solutions, as demonstrated by the explosion in high-security residential complexes modelled on the North American *gated communities*. In short, it may well be that our societies are becoming 'financially rich and humanly destitute', in the words of a European parliamentarian formerly very committed to the fight for human rights but now serving time for embezzlement.

The second decade of the millennium thus looks like being a period of almost guaranteed world prosperity, with the developed and newly industrialized countries taking the lion's share. The old Europe has had to adjust to the global trend, and even sets the pace in certain fields, but, this adjustment has been made at the cost of scaling down the social or environmental ideas advocated (if not always defended) by the Europeans of the last century. It is possible that future generations will not thank us for these years of prosperity and the liabilities (particularly environmental) we bequeath them. In the meantime, the machine continues to run at full throttle ...

2.   Scenario no. 2: the Hundred Flowers

'2000–2010: A decade without government' is the title given by *Everywhere's Citizens* to its special issue reviewing the first ten years of the century. This magazine – produced by a huge international association of the same name with millions of members: individuals, businesses and NGOs in all countries – is one of many examples of grassroots initiatives throughout the world. The weekly edition of this electronic publication reports on new experiments taking place, often on a modest scale, in a number of different fields ranging from commerce to culture, through welfare and environmental protection. Some observers are convinced that these burgeoning local projects signal the beginnings of a global participative democracy; the process is in fact completely rudderless, and the world is settling into an unstable equilibrium over which neither governments nor multinationals have any influence, given their dearth of room for manoeuvre and lack of legitimacy. Economic performance is disappointing on the whole, even relative to the diminished expectations of the end of the twentieth century. The increasingly uneven distribution of wealth, the proliferation of international crime and the multiplication of small regional conflicts are destabilizing the global system, but it still continues to muddle along. Europe, for its part, is evolving just as patchily as its partners. Some regions have sunk into a lethargy from which it seems they will never rouse themselves, while others are forging ahead with remarkable vitality and enthusiasm: under the leadership of a new generation of business people, and taking full advantage of the access to knowledge offered by the new technologies, cities and whole regions are enjoying an unprecedented economic, cultural and social revival. Bogged down in their obsolete ways of working, the administrations and political systems of the capital cities have not been able to stay abreast of these 'micro-Renaissances' and have slowly lost touch with the real world. By contagion, the European Union too is losing more and more of its powers of persuasion and has seriously undermined its credibility by abandoning half-way its planned expansion eastwards.

On closer scrutiny, the first signs of the decline of public authorities in Europe could have been discerned back in the early 1980s. What was considered at the time to be a temporary blip in fact masked an irreversible weakening of old-style government and old-mode administrative organization. Rigid hierarchies, the compartmentalization of competencies and excessive confidence in scientific expertise had sown the seeds of a widespread lack of responsibility, leading to the squandering of resources and the (at times tragic) mistakes of the end of the last century. At a time when societies were growing in complexity, technological innovation was gathering pace and individual needs were becoming increasingly differentiated, bureaucracies remained inflexible and unable to adjust to increasingly varied situations. Aware of the problem, governments reacted in a frenzy of mini-reforms which merely made matters worse: far from prompting a radical re-think of the entire system, this tinkering took up a large share of civil servants' time and energy, at the expense of their basic tasks. Constantly showered with unworkable schemes, the administrations rose to new levels of incoherence.

These daily malfunctions exacerbated the deep-seated dissatisfaction which the public was already harbouring with regard to the political and economic system. Faced with this malaise, political circles displayed an in-built inability to provide any answers: the debate alternated between abstraction and populism, and was sustained by a diet of never-ending corruption scandals, against which the law often proved powerless. At regular intervals governments would call for self-sacrifice in the name of budget austerity: to reach the 'inescapable paradise' held out by globalization, increased taxes on labour and consumption had to be accepted (since they claimed that other resources, particularly income from capital, had become too footloose). From the 1980s onwards, the European public had been showing increasing signs of unease, most often in referenda or elections and occasionally by joining spontaneous movements such as the 'white march' held in Brussels in autumn 1996. By 2000 and 2001, which were rich both in political scandals and in redundancies in sectors of the economy that had been spared up to that point, cynicism reached new heights: at the turn of the century, the public no longer expected anything either from politicians or from big businesses, which could get away with reporting their best profits of the decade and announcing further downsizing in the space of a few days.

This total lack of confidence sparked off the political and social crisis of 2000–2005. Lawsuits, product boycotts and sabotage proliferated, ensnaring big businesses and administrations in legal tangles from which they were unable to extricate themselves. Faced with mass abstention by voters and elected on low turnouts, national and regional governments lost their legitimacy. Above all, disregard for authority took root and the people increasingly took matters into their own hands, to varying degrees in different countries: hundreds of citizens' action groups were set up, some to stop the building of new motorways or the closure of local public services, others to boycott, sabotage or drag before the courts large corporations accused of misleading advertising, unethical behaviour or over-use of international transport and genetically modified ingredients. Banks were hit by endless boycotts for speculating on the stock market or not caring about small customers. The spread of direct action, tax evasion, absenteeism, the underground economy and non-observance of administrative formalities brought the system to a standstill.

Many contemporary observers were taken aback by the stoicism with which people seemed to cope with the crisis. From the 1990s, Europeans had in fact already begun withdrawing into the underground economy, their families and the local community, and this trend gathered pace at the end of the century: the underground economy, including undeclared labour, already accounted for a good fifth of the GDP of some EU Member States before the crisis. Above all, basic forms of social solidarity re-emerged at around the same time all across Europe: barter, skills exchanges, neighbourhood networks, to name but a few. During the crisis, people took up leisure activities with a productive aim, such as growing vegetables and do-it-yourself. The consumer goods market saw a spectacular influx of craft products, accompanied by a growing second-hand trade. Most of all, new shared values emerged, a somewhat nostalgic blend of local action, good-neighbourliness, mutual support and a return to nature. The grandchildren of the consumer society discovered with interest that fish were not born rectangular, frozen and breaded.

This period saw the rise of vigorous local communities as we know them today. It is rare nowadays to find a district or borough that does not have its own currency and a skills exchange where people can trade private tuition, cultural activities and all kinds of personal services (e.g. remedial schooling, child-care, home help, care for the elderly). Local associations, often run by women, pensioners or young graduates, have mushroomed and turned into *de facto* small businesses. Most of these operate on an unofficial basis, not bothering to register with the relevant authorities or pay taxes. Some, with help from the local council, play an important role in granting petty loans to individuals and small businesses that need small amounts quickly. Others have set up 'community money chests' to fund financial-support networks and, when the need arises, even provide grants for study or retraining. The more advanced might pay out welfare benefits. In other places, new-style local trade unions have been formed to defend the rights of inhabitants in general as well as those of workers. A large majority of these local community structures have remained very open to the outside world. Making full use of information technology (without which most of them would never have come into existence at all), they have developed international communication, partner-ships and exchanges of experience, not only between EU countries but also with partners in Eastern Europe, the Mediterranean and Africa.

The European economy too has undergone far-reaching changes. More in tune with people's needs, the local economy is gradually superseding the consumer society. Having seen sales plummet during the crisis years, supermarkets and large shopping centres re-oriented their sales policies to afford a higher profile to local production, organic foods, and cultural goods. The consumer durables industry (cars, household appliances) likewise had to adjust to the fall in demand and satisfy new consumer requirements for products that are robust and easy to repair. Given the unpopularity of the most heavily standardized goods, businesses have diversified their sales and advertising strategies, often down to regional level. At the same time, there has been steady growth in demand for all kinds of other goods and services: environmental protection, leisure, culture, and in general all products related to information and knowledge. The knowledge industry and the information technologies have in fact become the most dynamic sectors of the European economy. Like everywhere else in the world, the number of users continues to rise, and this growth should be boosted by the arrival of whole generations for whom the computer's everyday role in work, play, communication and culture is taken for granted. With the break-up of big businesses, the proliferation of small production units and the rising importance of self-employment, the needs of customers are increasingly catered for locally, and this boom in made-to-measure goods and services is another factor which makes for increasing use of information technology. At the same time, the IT industry has adjusted to shifts in demand by developing less technically sophisticated products that are affordable for most people and have longer life cycles. Demand from non-expert users is booming, and associations, knowledge banks, neighbourhood organizations, local webs and the like have all demonstrated an insatiable appetite for modern means of communication and access to knowledge.

For the rest, European businesses have shaken off many legal and administrative constraints. The European economy can in fact be said to have become self-regulating. Like the Internet, it is mainly governed by voluntary agreements between users and service providers: producers set themselves stringent standards of quality and transparency in order to win public confidence and avoid the boycotts regularly called by NGOs and consumer groups. Everywhere, the public authorities' control over economic life is being rolled back. In two or three of the smallest and most efficiently run countries, the role of the public authorities was scaled down at the initiative of the governments and social partners, who undertook a negotiated simplification of the tax system and social legislation. Elsewhere, the economy was deregulated *de facto*, through the combined effect of globalization and the undermining of public authority. The rules, for example the requirements of labour legislation, remain in force on paper, but their complexity, the dearth of checks, and the 'flexibility' of inspectors mean that businesses have plenty of latitude in applying them. The boundaries between legitimate business, the informal economy and petty corruption are furthermore becoming increasingly blurred.

Economists estimate that the undergound economy represents around 30 per cent of GDP in Europe (up to 50 per cent in some Member States!). Alongside traditional undeclared work, demonetization accounts for the sharp increase in recent years: a growing share of economic activity, and notably trade in basic goods and services, relies on barter and local currencies.

The extreme fragmentation of the economy has greatly contributed to worsening social and geographical inequalities. If statistics are to be believed, the most advanced regions and the big cities are far richer than the others in terms of wealth per inhabitant, and the gaps are steadily widening. However, these figures no longer paint a true picture of the standard of living: the poorer regions are also those where the informal economy is most highly developed, and the *quality* of life would seem to be higher in rural areas to judge by the number of young pensioners who decide to retire to the countryside. Also, although redistribution systems are less generous and more incoherent than they were last century, they continue to hand out considerable amounts. Despite the austerity policies introduced by governments, it is still easy without being particularly astute to take advantage of the many mistakes, procedural ambiguities and inconsistencies in the rules and criteria. Europeans have thus developed the habit of filling in forms as if they were playing the lottery, in the hope of winning the odd benefit or allowance: more and more people, for example, are only bothering to work for as long as it takes to re-establish their entitlement to unemployment benefits. Such confusion is perhaps not very rational, but it allows many to make ends meet, and we are seeing, in some urban areas, the emergence of a new 'poor leisured class'.

It is even more difficult to develop a coherent overview of the political map of Europe: here too, the leitmotiv is fragmentation. Generally speaking, the large countries were hardest hit by the crisis facing the administrations, and their capital cities have lost much of their ascendancy. Localities with strong economic and cultural foundations have made the most of these changing conditions and established their autonomy more firmly still: some are pursuing policies and engaging in diplomatic activities worthy of sovereign states. Other regions, unable to take advantage of their newly found freedom, are hamstrung by dependence on special interests and by clan quarrels, that is if they have not quite simply fallen under the control of a large local firm or mafia. The smaller Member States have often come out best: those which were traditionally the most highly decentralized and the least bureaucratic more or less weathered the storm, while at the other end of the spectrum, those which had for years been suffering from serious malfunctions collapsed completely, in some cases prompting their most prosperous regions to secede. All in all, the political geography of Europe in 2010 is a bizarre patchwork of principalities, city states, fiefdoms and a few small nation states which survived the upheaval at the beginning of the century.

Above this uneven landscape hovers a somewhat shadowy European Union. In actual fact, European integration was badly hit by the political crisis: faced with constant erosion of their legitimacy, the governments of the early years of the century were not conspicuous in their concern for long-term issues and tended to scale down their ambitions for Europe. Eastward enlargement no doubt provides the best illustration of this: by 2001–2002, it became clear that public opinion in some countries was afraid that extension of the Union towards Central and Eastern Europe would lead to worse unemployment and a rise in organized crime. Governments carefully avoided opening up the issue to public debate. They were prolific in anxious statements and fertile in diplomatic initiatives that slowed down the process, for example re-opening *ad infinitum* discussions on the cost of enlargement or calling for countless reports on the applicant countries and their degree of preparedness. This behaviour in no way mitigated the mistrust of the general public, but undoubtedly contributed to a souring of relations between the Union and its neighbours. Faced with this new set of hurdles, only four countries managed to stay on course and join the Union. The other applicant countries were weakened for many years to come: exhausted by 15 years of sacrifice and economic injustice, their populations were no longer prepared to listen to promises of a brighter future. Reforms stagnated, economic activity and investment ran out of steam, and Central and Eastern Europe sank into long-term economic and political instability.

With hindsight, it is fair to say that the Union itself is still paying a high price for the failure of enlargement. For one thing, it has lost its credibility on the international scene for a long time to come and has alienated its close neighbours: the peoples of Central and Eastern Europe feel that other Europeans, including the new Member States, have abandoned them to their fate, and their governments loudly proclaim at every opportunity that joining the Union is no longer one of their priorities, while at the same time endeavouring to build bilateral diplomatic alliances with the large Member States, particularly Germany. Then again, the instability of the neighbouring countries creates direct threats to the Union's security. The gravest of all at the present time is international crime, which is tightening its hold on the countries of Central Europe and spilling over into the Member States which share borders with them. But if the region's economic prospects remain as bleak as they are now, we will probably see a deterioration of relations between the Central and Eastern European countries themselves which could lead to a resurgence of ethnic or environmental disputes, notably in the Balkans and the Mediterranean. Lastly, on the economic front, businesses that were gearing up to enter new markets in the wake of enlargement have reined in their enthusiasm and cut back their investment programmes.

Unfortunately, enlargement is not the only area where the European Union has suffered from the deterioration in the political climate at home. Europe's political integration has made little progress over the last 15 years. The Common Foreign and Security Policy has not moved forward a single inch on paper, and has tended rather to lose ground in practice. The larger Member States, especially the Franco-German duo, no longer agree on strategic priorities: Berlin is focusing exclusively on Central Europe, whereas Paris appears to be preoccupied above all with the Mediterranean. In these circumstances, common foreign policy projects become bogged down in budget disputes, the Member States keep loudly announcing initiatives that never get off the ground, and the Union hardly ever presents a united front except during trade negotiations (and then only to take up an increasingly protectionist stance). Co-operation in the field of justice and home affairs is also at a standstill. Despite growing concern about organized crime, there is little hope for early progress on that front given the extent to which national law-enforcement and judicial systems are disorganized ... and Mafia-style networks have infiltrated Europe itself. According to a well-known judge, interviewed recently by one of the leading European dailies, the EU's inactivity could also be explained by the way in which the election campaigns of certain Heads of Government are financed. On the economic front, the Euroland countries are preserving their monetary and budgetary stability but only thanks to constant 'creative accounting'. As for the Single Market, the rules remain consistent on paper, although no one is really interested in checking that they are applied properly in practice. In the final analysis, optimists believe that, despite its ups and downs, the European venture is still moving forward, while pessimists proclaim that the only integration that still exists in practice is that of Mafia groups. The two Nordic countries that recently announced their intention of leaving the EU seem to share the latter view.

Despite appearances, the situation in Europe is in fact neither worse nor better than in other parts of the world: there is no escape from political and ethnic fragmentation, economic slowdown and increased tensions due to competition for natural resources. The United States is mostly bound up with its domestic problems but maintains a minimum presence on the world stage through its special relationships with China and Latin America. It defends its trading interests uncompromisingly, and occasionally indulges in a little risk-free diplomatic gesturing or military action against small rebellious countries (such interventions generally being well timed for domestic political purposes). The Asian countries are not succeeding in making headway towards regional integration, and their concerns are even tending to diverge: China's priority, for example, is to quell its violent domestic tensions caused by thirty years of unbalanced development. The extent of regional divergences makes one doubt that the country will survive as a single entity by the middle of the century. Finally, Russia alternates signs of recovery to relapses into chaos: it is re-establishing trade and diplomatic links with Central and Eastern Europe and reinforcing its bilateral relationship with the USA, but it remains above all a major source of disorder in Europe. All in all, it is quite possible that the world is becoming slowly caught in a vicious circle: weakened by their domestic problems, the regional powers are unable to instil any logic into the world system or the international institutions, a fact which is aggravating the global political and economic situation and feeding domestic tensions everywhere. That said, to quote a recent remark by the UN Secretary General, 'there are historical situations in which an unstable equilibrium seems able to last a thousand years'.

Or is what we are witnessing in fact the beginnings of a grass-roots renaissance? After visiting Europe last year, a famous Chinese painter published a travel book in which he described at length the enthusiasm and optimism he had come across in most of its cities and regions. He concluded in the following terms: 'Although I am no gardener, I can assure you that never has a tree died with such vivacious roots. I wager that they will need less than five years to restore it to life right to its uppermost branches'.

3.   Scenario no. 3: Shared Responsibilities

Those who predicted an apocalyptic third millennium for the *old world* will not be remembered for their clairvoyance. Europe has undergone profound changes over the past 15 years. In a favourable world economic climate it has found a way of reconciling its ideals of solidarity and respect for the individual with technological innovation and the pursuit of economic efficiency. The explanation for this change undoubtedly lies in the transformation of the public sector: after ten years of ambitious reforms the political authorities and administrations have become facilitators or partners, helping individuals, firms and civic associations to assume their share of responsibility for the life of the community. As European Union Heads of State or Government talk of starting accession negotiations with Turkey, the Union can congratulate itself on the success of the enlargement to include Cyprus and Central and Eastern Europe – and on its ability to carry out this operation at the same time as taking political integration a step further. Thanks to the extensive public debate and the reforms of recent years, the European public has embraced integration. This has conferred greater legitimacy on the Union, and as a result substantial progress has been made in such areas as social affairs and environmental protection. Having shaken off its twentieth-century attitudes, the Union has also become more self-assured in its relations with the rest of the world: it has forged solid political partnerships with its neighbours and the other major regional organizations in the world, calling constantly for better international co-operation and an ambitious reform of UN institutions. As the EU President put it recently: 'Europe is ageing rather well, at least for the time being'.

Exactly when these reforms began is still the subject of sterile debate among academics and journalists. In reality, the foundations of the major transformation of the first decade had been laid a long time ago. In fact, references to principles of individual responsibility, openness, decentralization of public services, and so on, started to crop up in the speeches of most European political leaders back in the 1980s. All Member States were carrying out experiments in consultation, involving the public in decision-making, etc., in some cases as early as the 1960s. At EU level, the Maastricht and Amsterdam Treaties already contained declarations of intent for a stronger social Europe, greater emphasis on the civil society, the principles of openness and subsidiarity, and finally the 'closer co-operation' clause enabling the

Union to develop certain policies without those Member States that prefer to stand aside.

However, one could hardly discern an overall logic in what was going on. The general public was showing signs of discontent and they became increasingly resentful at being presented with *faits accomplis* by the traditional alliance of technocrats and political leaders. By the end of the century, a climate of profound mutual distrust prevailed between the political classes and the ordinary citizens of the continent. At the same time, those working at grassroots level were demanding more responsibility: local authorities, associations, organizations defending the rights of the socially excluded. All were demanding a greater say in public decisions and a direct role in their implementation. They seemed to be expecting the governments and the political leaders to play an active role as facilitators, creating the necessary forums for debate and dialogue, defending a clear vision of where common interest lies and pushing for solutions acceptable to all.

In various ways, this pernicious climate was reigning everywhere in Europe, but it affected Brussels even more than the national capitals. In the face of growing criticism, the European institutions embarked in 1999–2000 on a series of wide-ranging evaluations of the way Community policies were implemented by the Commission, the regions and national administrations. The review revealed a few clear-cut cases of dishonesty, but above all an impression of extraordinary confusion: between geographical levels, between departments of the same administration, between regulations. The examples and the seriousness of the problem varied according to subject matter and country: in some places the Union and the Member States ran policies that were complementary on paper but contradictory in practice; elsewhere, there was so little consultation between central and regional authorities that procedures proliferated, with much duplication. Elsewhere again, the circulation of information between the ministries of one country, or the Directorates General of a single administration, left much to be desired. In some Member States, accounting and financial procedures were both slow and incapable of preventing the misuse of public funds. Although the problem varied in degree, the conclusion was the same everywhere: the system was plagued by inconsistencies that served nobody's interests.

A Committee of Wise Men charged with conducting comprehensive review of ways of improving the situation reported to the Västervik European Council in June 2001. Its report, entitled *Coordinating, Encouraging, Facilitating: the Role of the Public Sector in the Twenty-first Century*, called for a thorough reorganization of the public authorities at local, national and Community level, according to four fundamental principles: decentralization and, wherever possible, delegation of responsibilities; openness and clarity of objectives; accountability and enforcement of commitments to quality;

subsidiarity, including the *duty* of co-operation between different levels of government. To help put these principles into practice, the Wise Men recommended turning the hierarchical pyramids on their heads: each level of government and administration serving the levels below, and all levels serving the citizen – whose right to information, consultation, transparency and access to justice was to be guaranteed by the Union, the Member States and the regions. The report proposed the introduction of a *code of conduct for public service* to be binding on all levels of administration. The Swedish Prime Minister gave a simple but enthusiastic welcome to the proposals: 'The only way forward for Europe is a revolution in everyday life, carried out by the majority. We have just set this revolution in motion in our administrations, the very heart of the state apparatus'.

The Västervik report received mixed notices, depending on the Member State. In some, the public sector unions called strikes as soon as the first implementing laws were passed. On the whole this radicalism went down badly with the public and ultimately played into the hands of reformers by marginalizing the most conservative groups. We soon saw the creation of associations of public servants who supported far-reaching change, particularly local officials, environmental officers and community welfare workers. These periods of tension left deep scars in some countries, but did not impede the smooth running of the process. By 2004 the reform of the administration was on a scale that made the efforts of the previous century look like amateurish tinkering

The Union and the Member States applied the principle of accountability to all their policies. In agriculture and industry, contracts have been introduced requiring the beneficiary to observe certain basic precepts, such as environmental protection, product quality and compliance with employment law. Regional policy has also been reorganized according to a system of regional contracts: regions define their priority objectives every five years so that the Union and the states can adjust and target their aid accordingly. In general, the principle of a reciprocal undertaking between the citizen and the State has taken root everywhere, even in areas that remain national or regional responsibilities (such as social welfare or education). The role of managers has also increased throughout the public service: in some countries, for example, the heads of educational establishments have the autonomy of a company manager, subject to compliance with an education charter (an annual contract tailored to the individual college and setting standards to be attained).

Governments did have to prove, however, that their new role of network co-ordinator produced results. They concentrated their efforts on reforming the economic system, and in particular cutting unemployment (which was the public's main concern). The first victories on the employment front came in

2002, when local employment pacts became standard practice. These pacts bring together local authorities, universities, employment agencies, businesses, community associations, workers, the unemployed, traders, pensioners, etc. in pursuit of a simple objective: ensuring a better recon- ciliation of their respective needs. Most of the time, they have allowed for greater flexibility in the workforce while safeguarding the employees' income stability and career prospects. In other cases, participants have taken the initiative of introducing charters on trading and working hours, aimed at improving the overall supply of services. Organizing these pacts has required a huge investment in time and energy on the part of the public authorities. Local and national administrations ensure that all stakeholders are fairly represented, they act as arbitrators in the discussions and, if necessary, join in the financing of projects. The EU is responsible for circulating information at European level to encourage wide adoption of the best practices. The overall impact of the employment pacts has been highly positive: by stimulating the supply of new services and innovations in products and organization, they have helped to absorb a certain amount of structural unemployment.

The *Partner State* approach has also changed the attitude of the public authorities to the world of business. In addition to their traditional tasks of regulating economic activity and competition, the public authorities are now engaged in more proactive industrial policies. Information technologies are probably the best example: at the end of the last century it became apparent that Europe could only develop this sector fully if the technologies went hand in hand with the profound change going on in societies and attitudes. Steps had to be taken, in conjunction with users and the industry, to identify future needs so as to adapt the technologies to societies, rather than importing ever more advanced technologies with no obvious added value to the user. Public intervention thus focused on subsidies for social research, support for pilot projects paving the way for new applications of the technology, and information on new practices.

Concerning social dialogue, important breakthroughs have taken place over the recent years thanks to the strong commitment of governments. In the field of labour law and social protection, better representation of young people, atypical workers and the socially excluded has helped to break the deadlock in relations between the social partners. In some countries the traditional unions managed to broaden their base and embrace the claims of groups in a less secure situation; in others new bodies emerged to represent specific interests. The appearance of these new delegates at the negotiating table had the effect of reducing the benefits enjoyed by those with traditional jobs (stable employment within a large organization), but helped to combat exclusion and reduce long-term unemployment. The decentralization of industrial relations also made it possible to take more account of regional and sectoral differences which, depending on the industry involved, can lead to quite significant differences between collective agreements.

In their reform of pension and health insurance schemes the Member States have also tried to reconcile the desire to maintain a high level of social protection with the need for greater flexibility and individual responsibility. The changes introduced in social security clearly illustrate this point: in a variety of ways Member States have all moved towards a 'one-stop shop' approach, whereby a contractual relationship can be established with the recipients of assistance, and abuse and inconsistencies between different rules reduced. In practice, this change has helped to reintegrate quite a large number of the socially excluded, but it does lead to what sociologists dub the 'tyranny of harmony' or the *Big Brother* syndrome: some people in difficulty are unable to sustain the contractual relationship and end up rejecting the psychological constraint and constant supervision to which they are subject. In the case of pensions, the system has evolved towards a more equitable distribution of income between the generations. Most Member States are beginning to reap the benefits of the reforms of the 1990s, such as the progressive deferment of the retirement age and the development of complementary private mechanisms. Those countries that were slower to tackle the problem now face a delicate financial balancing act in the next decade.

All in all, the last ten years have proved rather beneficial to Europe's competitiveness. Since the end of the twentieth century, the *old world*'s companies have enhanced their presence in high-technology markets, particularly the knowledge-related industry. Judging by the steady increase in foreign investment, the European economy seems well perceived from outside. Multinational firms and foreign observers apparently acknowledge the existence of a 'European way', in other words a higher involvement of the State and a permanent constraint on consultation and consensus building – but as a compensation the near certainty to reach 'win–win' solutions that could not be attained by other means than dialogue. Beyond this somewhat idyllic reading, many worry about a potential drift of the so-called 'European model' towards undue state interventionism and appalling complexity: the 'ideology of consensus' and the magma of rules and commitments it generates may well paralyse companies and public apparatuses as surely as the Lilliputians managed to tie up Gulliver ...

The recent evolution has given mixed results in terms of social and regional cohesion: the overall impact of the reforms has been positive, but it has fallen short of the expectations of the proponents of a social *third way*. Poverty and the gap between rich and poor have ceased to increase since 2005, but they have stabilized at a high level, at least in comparison with the halcyon days of the post-war era. What is more, governments have achieved this modest result at the cost of a slight increase in the number of individuals drawing their income directly or indirectly from public funds. Geographical inequalities have also started to recede, thanks to better differentiation of European aid according to the specific needs of each region. A 'cyclical stabilization instrument' has also been introduced, i.e. a system of aid triggered automatically when a region of the Union suffers an economic downturn (aid is granted in the event of a sudden fall in growth or a sharp rise in the region's unemployment rate). Nevertheless, economic prosperity continues to elude vast swathes of EU territory, and in some cases the situation has actually deteriorated since the reforms, often because the local public sector remains stubbornly old-fashioned (decentralization has in some cases exacerbated clientelism). With the tacit support of the Member States in question, the European Union may sometimes make the maintenance of its funding for these regions dependent on speeding up administrative reforms, although there have been cases where this sort of intervention has made matters worse rather than better.

As to the European societies themselves, the most striking feature over recent years has been the rise of civil society. The subsidies for social and political innovation introduced in most European regions have enabled many people to set up local community associations, networks for political debate, etc. These *active citizens* represent only a fifth of the population, but form an extremely dynamic network with, increasingly, a European dimension. Young people, women and pensioners play a major role in them. On the other hand, political life can hardly be said to arouse much enthusiasm beyond this active minority. The general public accepts the reforms with a sort of resigned fatalism, but opinion polls reflect a certain weariness, with the pace of change, the complexity of public life and the endless sacrifices (some social groups even manifest their dissatisfaction repeatedly, for instance the elderly, public sector employees and small businessmen). Sociologists also detect a growing propensity for boredom among young people, leading them to question the consensus and challenge half-measures – as well as growing interest for emigration among young businessmen. However, public opinion in Europe seems to be broadly united around values such as faith in the individual, solidarity and accountability, and lifestyles seem to be converging. A vast majority of Europeans are attached to the family (at least in its modern incarnation: small and in many cases spread out), they welcome the role played by women in the economy and public life, and they are broadly tolerant of other generations and ethnic, cultural and sexual differences.

The European Union, for its part, is still in the process of digesting the recent enlargement towards Central and Eastern Europe. As the Prague European Council prepares to debate the opening of negotiations on Turkish membership, the EU may be said to have successfully addressed the challenge: between 2004 and 2009 13 new states have joined the Union (Switzerland, Norway and Iceland dusted off their applications and two have become members). All Central and Eastern European countries are well on their way towards economic modernization, and some have even managed to climb their way from near bankruptcy to membership in the selective Euro-zone in less than twenty years. With some exceptions, the governments of the new Member States have also accomplished significant progress in the field of environment and social welfare – thanks to the constant pressure coming from Brussels and from public opinion.

The success of enlargement owes much to world economic prosperity and the relatively peaceful relations between the EU's neighbours, but it is also due to the constant commitment of the Member States and the gradual emergence of a common political vision. On this last point, matters had begun inauspiciously. At the end of the last century the national capitals seemed to nurse rather different ambitions for the Union, and the first enlargements to Central and Eastern Europe heightened this apparent divergence. Matters came to a head in 2005. The institutions were reaching saturation despite some changes introduced by a minor reform round at the beginning of the century – the Union was treading water on matters of major importance, such as foreign policy, and public opinion continued to question the legitimacy of the system.

Keen to clarify their common political vision and raise the EU's profile with ordinary people, the Member States took the initiative of organizing a huge continent-wide debate: the European Council asked a group of 60 people to formulate in half a year a vision for Europe, to serve as a basis for widespread public debate. The Coimbra Group consisted of men and women, workers, farmers, employees, artists, entrepreneurs, trade unionists, social workers, academics and political leaders from all Member States and applicant countries, reflecting most of Europe's political currents. It even included a top footballer. After completing their report, the *Kwik-Fix Club* (as the journalists dubbed them) spent a whole year presenting their conclusions to the widest possible audiences. Thanks to this strong media coverage, the work of the Coimbra Group prompted a high-quality democratic debate on the political blueprint for Europe and it heralded two major changes. First, it enabled the general public to get rid of the existential questions about whether they were 'for or against Europe' – and to really start considering the fundamental challenges that the continent had to face. Second, it demonstrated that Europeans actually demanded 'more Europe' and expected greater political clout, particularly in high-profile areas like internal security and foreign affairs. Hence, one can say that the work of the *Kwik-Fix Club* started the ball rolling for the major institutional reform that was conducted in 2007. The Heads of State decided to renounce unanimity voting across the board, to raise the Union's budget, to make the Economic and Social Committee more representative of civil society, to convoke randomly chosen samples of citizens to debate on issues of general interest (especially risks linked to science and technology) – and, last but not least, to strengthen the Court of Justice, now the sole interpreter for the subsidiarity principle. Among these ambitious reforms, few would ever have come to daylight without the major effort of reflection, debate and explanation that was undertaken by Coimbra.

The most considerable progress at Union level over the last years has been achieved in the field of foreign policy. The EU has emerged as a pre-eminent power in the region thanks to the ambitious political partnerships it has developed with its whole neighbourhood. To the South, the creation of OCOMED (Organization for Co-operation in the Mediterranean area, which brings together the Commission, the 28 Member States and all the states of the Mediterranean basin) has given a new dimension to the Euro-Mediterranean partnership in terms of resources invested and areas of activity. The partnership now covers widely different fields, from military matters and support for democracy to the proliferation of contacts between community associations and private industry on either side of the Mediterranean. To the East, the EU has developed far-reaching co-operation with its three big neighbours, placing special emphasis on areas of common interest such as the fight against organized crime and illegal immigration networks. For two of these countries these special ties should ultimately lead to membership. In the case of Turkey the possibility of opening negotiations will be discussed at the next European Council, and Ankara's conciliatory line on the Cypriot question and respect for human rights should overcome the reluctance which persists in certain capitals. As for Ukraine, the Union's High Representative recently recalled Ukraine's legitimate aspiration to join the 'Twenty-Eight' as soon as its economy is capable of facing the competition within the Single Market.

However, the EU's influence goes beyond its immediate neighbours. At international level it is now the self-styled defender-in-chief of the multilateral institutions: the Union likes to argue that the global system will be effective only if it is balanced and able to take into account the specific characteristics and interests of all the states involved (to quote the High Representative again, 'if it is to serve everyone, the system of international institutions must not serve anyone individually'). This attitude has occasionally led to tension with the United States, but has revealed some common ground with states like China, India, Russia and Brazil, all of which would like to play a full part in the international system on condition that they have a say in the establishment of its rules and principles. More generally, the Union is making its voice heard more clearly in defence of its own values, particularly the social dimension, individual rights and sustainable development. It has even won admiration on several occasions by ostentatiously imposing stricter standards on itself than its partners, for example in environmental protection.

For all this, with the exception of the occasional spectacular event, the international system remains fragile, and considerable powers of persuasion will be needed to arrive at an effective joint management of major global risks. In the meantime, the trend everywhere in the world is towards a reinforcement of regional constituencies, of which the Union itself is the most accomplished example so far (explaining why it is occasionally quoted as a model). Most of the world's major regions have made significant progress towards closer co-ordination, in the economic field as well as in more political areas like crisis management, environment protection or soft security. In South-East Asia, co-operation between ASEAN, Japan and China (under the latter's leadership) has gained consistency in recent years, paving the way for a possible regional integration in some areas (China's and Japan's Prime Ministers recently announced that the time was ripe to start reflecting on the feasibility of an East Asian common currency). The renewed momentum in favour of South American integration or the dynamism of organizations such as the OAU all contribute to the emergence of an intermediary level of governance between the states and the international organizations. Russia and the United States also seem favourable to that trend. With its economic recovery fully on track, Russia still pursues a three-pronged diplomatic strategy aimed at reinforcing its presence in the multilateral institutions, consolidating the CIS and continuing its rapprochement towards the EU – to which Russia is now linked by a free-trade agreement. As far as the United States is concerned, it is still the world's major power but it starts measuring its interest in a more co-operative approach to world affairs (among other things, it seems to condone the integration initiatives taking place in South America, although these projects have mainly been developed independently of Washington).

Europe seems, thus, to be on the right track and is establishing its reputation as the doyenne of international relations. However, the next few years are likely to be at least as difficult as the decade 2000–2010: Europeans will need plenty of imagination and energy to maintain their position in the world economy, promote ideas of sustainable development, help Russia integrate completely into the international system and so on. More generally, the central role of the State in European societies remains a source of considerable dynamism, but the proliferation of pacts, charters and informal agreements of all kinds could easily degenerate into utter confusion – or become as complex and inefficient as the old welfare state at the end of the twentieth century. In the case of the European Union, although there are plenty of reasons for self-congratulation, its institutions are struggling to work with 28 members and it still has to cope with 12 new applicants. In an allusion to Airbus's latest jumbo aircraft, journalists have dubbed this prospective Union the 'EU 3XX'. We can only hope that it enjoys a following wind and that its 680 million passengers do not tire of the hyperactivity of the past few years ...

4.   Scenario no. 4: Creative Societies

Keynes feared the advent of the affluent society. 'Must we not expect a general "nervous breakdown"? ... For we have been trained too long to strive and not to enjoy.' With hindsight we can see that Europe did indeed suffer from this malaise, and the wave of strikes and urban unrest at the turn of the century could easily be mistaken for a continent-wide nervous breakdown. Disaster seems to have been averted, but it is still too soon to say whether the ambitious reforms of 2005–2006 will deliver the brighter future promised or whether they have set Europe for ever on the road to decline. In the eyes of their supporters, who remain in the majority, the reforms have returned man to his rightful place at the heart of economic development and laid the foundations for a new social solidarity, based on a new ethic of human quality and individual fulfilment and on a rejection of the materialism and obsession with productivity of the twentieth century. To others, the continent that was once the cradle of Western civilization is well and truly dead, the victim of its inability to grasp reality and its refusal to adapt to international economic constraints.

The social situation in Europe at the end of the last century was verging on the absurd. The gap between rich and poor was widening and the television news ran stories of soaring stock market profits alongside reports of poverty, despair and outright revolt. Governments finally put unemployment top of their list of priorities but seemed unable to translate their words into deeds. It took only a wave of mergers or downsizing to wipe out the few thousands of jobs created at great cost in tax breaks and government subsidies. As job security and stability declined, individuals longed above all for a better quality of life, for an economy that was attentive to their personal development and the environment, while the world of business seemed increasingly remote from these concerns.

In this difficult climate governments tried repeatedly to cut unemployment and social security benefits in a bid to stimulate recruitment and reduce labour costs. As a result of the budget overshoots and international recession of the start of the century, business circles and experts persuaded several EU governments to announce new austerity measures in early 2002. The response, as we all know, was unanimous: by March, half of Europe had taken to the streets. General strikes were called in France, Belgium, Italy, then Germany, Spain, the United Kingdom and Poland. Inner cities in Britain and Germany were the scene of violent clashes between the young unemployed and the police. In Essen a company chairman was lynched by employees after announcing redundancy plans. In Paris, Brussels, Rome, Bucharest and Warsaw open revolt broke out. Stock markets tumbled and currencies crashed, Switzerland agreed to take in a few fortunate refugees, and pictures of the Berlaymont in flames and the Italian President fleeing the Quirinale by helicopter under a hail of petrol bombs dominated front pages all over the world for weeks on end.

From Mondorf-les-Bains (Luxembourg), where the European Parliament had taken refuge, 150 MEPs issued a solemn appeal for a European Forum, a sort of cyber-States-General where people could voice their grievances and submit their proposals to save the situation. The Mondorf appeal called for 'a rediscovery of the human dimension' and stressed the need to change the world of work and 'give everyone the right to be useful other than through the pursuit of productivity alone'. The initiative received huge media coverage and was instrumental in restoring calm, once governments had pledged to organize the necessary regional and national forums. Some governments, bowing to public pressure, had to promise elections as soon as the debates were finished.

The Forums confirmed the need to give everyone, if not a job, then at least alternative means of ensuring a decent income, a minimum level of security and recognition of their social worth. The public's contributions also revealed the existence of numerous unsatisfied needs, in the form of services to families and the elderly or, quite simply, the desire of millions of individuals to develop their knowledge, personality and imagination. Many participants, young and old, economically active or marginalized (two terms almost never used nowadays), voiced their anger at a world where everything seemed to be for sale and where relations between individuals were becoming more and more impersonal because of lack of time, social interaction and trust. The Forums provided a platform for groups whose voices were not usually heard: young people, women, the excluded, small businesses. They received a total of 100 million written contributions and e-mails. The process showed that Europeans had plenty of ideas for improvements but felt hampered by the prevailing ideology and bureaucratic red-tape. After the whingeing tone of the first phase, the Forums developed into real arenas for debating solutions. To varying degrees and in different organizational frameworks, depending on the individual country, people all over Europe spent a whole year discussing questions like solidarity and sharing, the new needs of individuals, plans for a basic income for all, and constitutional reform. Governments and trade unions kept a low profile during the debates, but helped with the organization and agreed to a candid assessment of the weaknesses of the old system.

To say that the subsequent reforms were the work of the Forums would be an exaggeration. In fact the Forums acted more as a safety valve: as well as helping to restore order, they gave the public a chance to vent its anger – and the rulers and technocrats a better idea of the alienation felt by some of their fellow citizens. The riots and the Forums created extra popular pressure which can still be felt today and which explains both the spectacular internal changes of the last ten years and the top priority given by Member States of the Union to social questions, often at the expense of foreign policy.

Not content with merely tinkering to correct the most blatant inconsistencies, governments undertook a root-and-branch reform of the accounting and fiscal systems. To quote the Mondorf appeal, we had to 'learn to count what really counts', in other words to rework public and private accounts to include human capital and the environment. Since 2006 every firm or administration operating in Europe has been required to maintain green accounts and present an environmental impact assessment of its operations at the end of the year. The tax structure has been overhauled, and a full range of new taxes introduced on capital, international financial movements, pollution, energy and environmental damage. In exchange, labour and consumption received some relief from the high rates of tax suffered in the past. For the sake of efficiency, the Member States have agreed on European harmonization of tax rates and mechanisms for the most mobile resources (company profits, income from capital and financial movements), prompting the Commission President to comment at the end of the Luxembourg European Council of 2004 that, 'We have finally invented intelligent fiscal subsidiarity'. The European Union also introduced a tax on financial transactions in the euro zone, despite fierce opposition from the international business world and the reservations of economic experts.

The other great innovation of the first decade of the new millennium was the recognition and funding of types of activity that offer an alternative to traditional work. All Europeans were given the right to devote several years of their working life to collectively useful tasks that would not find a buyer in a strict market economy: services of general interest, cultural events, work in non-profit-making associations, services for the poor or even rearing children. This entitlement has been set at five years full-time throughout the Union. It is left to individuals to decide how to split this time up over their lifetime, depending on their plans and commitments (some will prefer to take periods of sabbatical leave, others will continue to work but will set aside a third or a quarter of their time for non-remunerable activities). Depending on the country, between 7 and 15 per cent of Europeans are taking advantage of this facility. The practical arrangements and funding conditions also vary from country to country: some states have opted for local funding by regional and local governments, companies and employers, others have introduced a system of tax allowances, etc. In general, the counterpart of these reforms has been a (downwards) revision of pension benefits and the statute of public sector workers. The 2005 European Directive on lifelong working-time management provides for easy mobility between the business, public and non-profit sectors and periods of training and sabbatical – by guaranteeing universal social protection, thereby removing the risks of discontinuity in health insurance when people's economic status changes. This legislation was welcomed by firms who saw it as a way of introducing greater flexibility at work, while avoiding personal hardship. Finally, to stimulate demand for new goods, most Member States have introduced systems of vouchers for services, leisure and culture known as *Clocs* from their French acronym and *EuroClocs* now that they have been harmonized across Europe). Europeans now receive on average 20 per cent of their revenue in the form of vouchers, regardless of whether they are employed, retired or receiving state benefit.

These reforms have achieved their main purpose, namely to improve the social situation. Europeans may be financially less well off than they were 20 years ago, but Europe has regained a level of *full activity*. The pensioners and the marginalized of the last century have found a useful role in society once again, and some deprived areas are experiencing a frenzy of artistic and cultural activity. Collective goods are a matter of constant concern, particularly the improvement of the living environment (to quote the mayor of a large town in Britain, 'it's as if the dealers have all moved into city beautification'). Organized protests have become mose rare, the last big demonstration being in 2006 when French pensioners protested against the conversion of part of their pensions into *Clocs*. Pensioners are often active protagonists in the service sector, and some are finally seeing their dreams of 1968 come true (on a more prosaic level, many Member States froze pensions in 2003 and activity allowances help people to make ends meet). On the whole, social and geographical inequalities have ceased to increase.

The economic impact is more debatable. The first years of the century were gloomy on the economic front, a low point being reached in 2003–2005 when negative average growth was recorded for the Union as a whole for two years in succession. Since the reforms, Europe has experienced an unprecedented contraction of its industrial base. The decline has been particularly marked in the polluting industries, despite the fact that some industrialists have consciously chosen to maintain production sites near their markets, even if it means adopting greener technologies. The major banks have also decided to relocate some of their activities abroad to evade, at least partially, the new taxes on financial transfers. On the whole, business leaders, including small businesses, had a hard time of it in the early years of the century and denounced the unrealistic aims of the social reformers. Their lack of confidence was reflected in financial stonewalling and the flight of some of

Europe's capital, at least provisionally, to more exotic accounts and investments.

The situation now shows signs of improving and some forecasters are predicting that by 2015 Europe will have regained the level of wealth it enjoyed at the turn of the century. Others even claim that it has already made up the lost ground if the new criteria of quality of life and collective goods are taken into account. The economic recovery has been led by the service sector, which now spans a much broader range, and in particular by knowledge and creativity industries (education and knowledge services, entertainment and cultural productions), environmental protection services and tourism. The most innovative firms have also taken advantage of the accounting reforms which allow them to treat certain training costs as investment in their human capital. In general, the private sector is beginning to benefit from the greater flexibility in employment contracts, the dynamism generated by work in the non-cash economy and the more efficient use of human capital. Some European companies are even taking the lead in creativity worldwide, and if Europe continues at the pace of the past few years it will register more patents per head of population than the United States or Japan by the year 2020. To complete the good news, the exchange rate of the euro has risen close to 1 US dollar, and a number of creative figures, artists and firms have recently moved to Europe from elsewhere, a trend which should gather momentum over the next few years. Most are apparently attracted by the quality of life, the atmosphere conducive to innovation and the creativity of the workforce. It is still too early to say whether these few swallows will really make a summer.

The internal economic situation may not be entirely rosy, but it is from outside the Union that the greatest difficulties can be expected in the years to come. Europe may pay a high price for its neglect of foreign policy questions since the turn of the century, and particularly of its role as a regional power. The years of unrest and social reform were incomprehensible to Central and Eastern Europe: with the exception of two countries that tentatively imitated the trend, public opinion in the applicant countries was out-of-tune with the green and red radicalism of Western Europe. The result was to delay enlargement: the first Central and Eastern European countries did not join the Union until 2008, and negotiations with the others are likely to take a few more years yet. The Union particularly tarnished its reputation by its blatant disregard for the applicant countries: while its social and environmental demands became stricter from one European Council to the next, it failed to introduce new aid mechanisms, and its Central European partners inevitably perceived the new criteria as further pretexts for delaying their accession.

European integration in general is looking somewhat shaky. This might seem paradoxical given that the Heads of State and Government are almost all on the same ideological wavelength, with the exception of two or three who came to power in the period of counter-revolutionary disillusionment that followed the Forums in their countries. In fact, the Member States look more to the short term, and their desire to produce rapid results sometimes leads them to hijack the European agenda. Generally, political control of the Community institutions has increased thanks either to the governments (control of the Central Bank, for example) or to NGOs, which are increasingly represented on the various working committees and in the Economic and Social Committee. Still, on average, the European institutions are functioning properly. Despite the unrest, Europe managed to keep the single currency afloat during the stormy early years of the century. The Forums may have been anathema to the euro, but not even the Member States least troubled by street protests ever seriously considered withdrawing from monetary union. The picture would not be complete without a mention of the extraordinary progress made in the field of co-operation in judicial, police and customs affairs, in response to growing public demand for security. Europol works well and has won its spurs cracking two European organized crime networks, one with close ties to certain governments. Illegal immigration is more or less under control, too, at the cost of massive reinforcement of customs and police controls that is hard to reconcile with the humanist and tolerant image that Europe likes to project to the rest of the world.

Immigration is just one of the areas in which Europe's deeds abroad fail to live up to its ideals. When the Member States manage to reach agreement, the European positions are more than ever subject to internal political compromises, and the Union is seen as less and less co-operative by the rest of the world, with the exception of countries like Canada and Japan, which at their own pace are starting to adopt social policies comparable to our own. There are good grounds for this view of Europe: in trade matters the 'Twenty-two' are undeniably developing a pronounced taste for protectionism and have on occasion used their 'social exception' to protect less competitive sectors. Even in areas where it likes to think of itself as progressive, such as human rights and sustainable development, the EU takes a pioneering position on selective issues but is not really developing a strategy for a thorough reform of the international economic order, for example. Matters could improve on this score, judging by the recent spate of alarmist declarations by NGO umbrella organizations and political leaders, like the recent statement by the European Commissioner for environment: 'Whether you like it or not, sustainable development is a global issue. Obviously we are all delighted that the forests are expanding every year in Europe. But how can a few extra trees here compete with the loss of the tropical rainforests?' One of the more interesting proposals is that the developed countries should pay the poorer countries to protect essential natural resources.

Besides sustainable development, international crime and world poverty are two other issues where a stronger system of international governance is urgently needed. Much will actually depend on the behaviour of the world's main powers over the next ten years – and whether they will seriously tackle the need for reinforcing multilateral co-operation. There is strong popular pressure in favour of such a process: in the most influential countries, the awareness of issues such as environmental degradation or world poverty is higher than ever. Canada and Japan have experienced a marked change in values over recent years, and signs pointing to the same direction are manifested throughout the developed world, notably in Oceania and the United States. In the US, the public shows signs of weariness and increasing resistance to the never-ending game of consumption and competition, and sociologists increasingly compare the situation there to Europe's at the beginning of the century. Still, with the exception of Europe and two or three other countries, the political élites of the developed world are not ready to make ecological and social questions an absolute priority – and foreign policy is the last field where they would contemplate doing so.

In the rest of the world, the situation remains unclear. East Asia has evolved in a piecemeal manner: Japan increasingly appears to go its own post-modern way, China's ambitions are hampered by economic difficulties and Beijing's resistance to any reform that would substantially alter the present political system, and the smaller countries are following different economic and political paths depending on how quickly they recovered from the economic crisis of the end of the 1990s. Closer to Europe, Russia remains beset by political and economic confusion, and it has to a large extent become estranged from the rest of the world, particularly its Western partners. As for the Mediterranean countries, they face the double challenge of demography and economic modernization with increasing difficulties. Resentment against the rich neighbours of the North is gaining ground, all the more since the EU does not pursue any coherent strategy towards the region (except for its restrictive immigration policy).

More generally, it becomes clearer every day that the Union's policy towards its neighbourhood cannot remain as inconsistent as it has been over the last ten years. The choice so far has been to intervene very little in regional quarrels, except to provide humanitarian assistance and aid for reconstruction and reform, and even here the EU's generosity is not on a par with the needs on the ground. As the failure of this *de facto* isolation strategy becomes blatant, EU governments try to convince their public opinions that the very survival of the European experience is in jeopardy. Indeed, unless Europe quickly understands the need to reinforce its international presence, the 'European social exception' might simply be remembered as unrealistic and ageing societies trying to build for themselves an illusory haven of peace and selfish prosperity. The prevailing mind-set is that the Union must devise urgently an ambitious neighbourhood policy, and there are even plans to gradually extend most EU policies and programmes (R&D, energy, environment ...) to a large Euro-Mediterranean area going from Russia to North Africa. This plan sounds far too ambitious to many, but it may well be the only way for European aspirations not to be swept away by the mere mechanics of demographic forces.

In short, depending on how the rest of the world evolves, Europe may have opened the way to a *Spiritual Renaissance* and shaped the values of a new, more co-operative world order serving human needs better. It remains to be seen whether it can command enough economic and intellectual power and count on enough allies to carry this mission through. Otherwise, Europe is simply closing itself off from the world and refusing the challenge of modernity – that it has done so much to shape but with which its people feel no affinity. As it is impossible to predict which way things will go let us instead consider the epigram delivered by the Argentine President on a recent visit to Brussels: 'Europe has certainly sparked off something. But it is hard to say whether it is a beacon for the rest of the world or a festive barbecue on shifting sands'.

5. Scenario no. 5: Turbulent Neighbourhoods

'Killed in action – for Europe.'

The recent Gdańsk European Council decided to erect, in every capital city, a white stone monument bearing these words in all the official languages of the Union, together with the names of the 10,000 soldiers who have died in action since the turn of the century. The special editions issued by Europe's press looking back on the first decade of the millennium, from 2000 to 2010, reveal just how preoccupied the Union has been with external matters. The European Security Council has deployed troops on four occasions to restore or maintain order in its own backyard. A preoccupation with security has become part of everyday life. The Eurovigil scheme, set up after the terrorist bombs in the spring of 2004, is the most obvious example, but it is just one sign of the fear Europeans feel towards the world beyond their borders and their anxiety about what the future holds for them. This siege mentality goes a long way towards explaining the stagnation in domestic policy: Member States' governments, particularly the larger ones, have won back much political capital with recent military successes, but not enough to convince an anxious public of the need for wide-scale economic and social reform. Over the past ten years, only two or three Member States have really stayed the course.

Twenty years after the end of the Cold War, political instability is a growing problem the world over, particularly in the countries neighbouring on Europe, and there is no indication that the situation will improve in the near future. Today's problem is the cumulative result of a number of converging and long-standing historical trends. The first real signs of environmental damage were visible way back in the twentieth century; sooner or later shortages of natural resources such as drinking water, and political struggles for control of them, were bound to follow. The splintering of the world political map and the rising number of local conflicts verging on civil war are not exactly recent phenomena either: the twentieth century saw the birth of over 150 new sovereign states (with a third of that figure in the last two decades alone!). Then came the end of the Cold War, which in some way had served to channel violence and keep the lid on minor conflicts around the globe. The system of alliances grouped around a limited number of major powers, notably the

United States and the Soviet Union, has broken down into a complex and less manageable tangle of networks, with ethnic guerrilla warfare, terrorism, organized crime and arms-dealing inextricably interlinked.

Lastly, economic globalization has not brought all the benefits promised by its most enthusiastic prophets: monetary instability is increasing, growth still slowing, and the rewards are unequally distributed, perpetuating global imbalances and reinforcing domestic social inequalities practically everywhere.

In the developed world, particularly the West, the public reacted to the end of the Cold War by losing interest in the rest of the world. In the absence of a direct and easily identifiable threat, governments and the public in Europe and the United States turned their attention to domestic policy issues. At the end of the century, though the West was moved by the images of war, massacres and genocide beamed to it from the Balkans and Africa, people's main concern was for a comfortable life, which was ultimately not threatened by those tragic events. The United States oscillated between relative withdrawal and the desire to maintain political prominence. Meanwhile, Europe relied on two apparent certainties: lasting peace between Member States (including those that were still just applicants) and the reassuring presence of the Atlantic Alliance.

In its state of genteel languor, the European public did not notice all the new military and soft security threats massing on the Union's doorstep. Yet all the makings of a crisis were already in place at the beginning of the century: a crumbling Middle East peace process, ethnic tensions in the Balkans and the eastern Mediterranean, and a gradually disintegrating Russia where organized crime was proliferating and hard-up generals were selling arms at knock-down prices. In addition, the natural environment all around the Union's rim was slowly but irreversibly deteriorating, with the over-exploitation of the Mediterranean coast to the south and massive industrial and agricultural pollution to the east. The first signs of genuine public concern came in 2002 following a minor nuclear incident in Central Europe and a wave of appalling famine in the former Soviet Union. Wrapped up in its own internal wrangles, the European Council termed 'unfeasible any form of political action that might lead to a lasting improvement in the situation in the affected countries'. This drew a certain amount of sarcastic comment from the press, though it was really just a reference to the extreme state of confusion in those countries. For example, a good deal of the humanitarian aid sent by the Union found its way into warehouses belonging to the local mafia, who promptly sold it on the black market. In the same year, the US Congress, strongly influenced by its more 'isolationist' members, published a report voicing concern about the growing instability in Europe and suggesting the time had come for the Europeans to 'shoulder the full burden of their security-related responsibilities, military and other'. When, on grounds of geopolitical instability, a number of credit-rating agencies nudged their ratings for European companies down a notch, stock markets showed signs of the jitters too.

From that time on, the Member States' governments were under constant pressure from the public and their main partners around the world: as the evidence of instability around its borders poured in, the Union was supposed to be devising a coherent and effective foreign policy. The Heads of State and Government managed to agree on a number of common foreign policy strategies: the Union tried to boost relations with the least stable countries in the region by proposing close political partnership on soft security matters, but the sheer force of events overwhelmed its efforts, and they did not produce any progress on more sensitive issues such as defence. This prompted the EU's foreign-policy supremo to say that 'the Member States continue to prefer national military weakness to European military strength'.

It was against this unsettled background that the 'Thirst War' broke out, just a few hundred kilometres from the Union's borders. At the height of summer in 2003, after two of its members had just been shot down by the police in a neighbouring country, a terrorist organization tipped several tankers of defoliant into a river near the border, effectively depriving all the towns downstream of drinking water. Riots followed, reviving ethnic tensions in the region and degenerating in a matter of weeks into a full-scale armed conflict, covertly supplied by a number of countries with varying ethnic, territorial and ideological designs. The war posed three major problems for the Union. First, it was impossible to implement an effective *cordon sanitaire* strategy. Second, it seemed likely that the region's large population would generate an uncontrollable flood of migrants and refugees. Above all, the ethnic militia groups fighting in the conflict had terrorist offshoots inside the Union. These cells proved their effectiveness over a bloody weekend in December 2003: on Saturday afternoon three car bombs exploded simultaneously on Regent Street, the Kurfürstendamm and the Champs-Elysées, killing hundreds of shoppers and injuring several thousand. The following week, France, Germany and the UK called an extraordinary meeting of the European Council, at which they announced plans to deploy ground troops with a mandate to 'restore peace by whatever means'. Faced with a *fait accompli*, most other EU governments decided to follow suit (just four chose not to, for reasons of neutrality or domestic policy). The same evening, the United States confirmed they would not be taking part in the operation and wished Europe good luck. Three weeks later, the first WEU contingents were on the ground. Six months and 25,000 deaths later, the Thirst War was over.

Without doubt, the deterioration in neighbourly relations and the events of winter 2003–2004 brought about profound changes in the European Union, particularly its institutions. Above all, security concerns have drastically limited the admission of new members: to quote the then Commission President: 'Europe ends where chaos and barbarism begin, and we have succeeded in saving most of Central Europe'. A common border-police force and a European intelligence service were set up (BordEuro and EuroSec), to which the 2006 Treaty of Gibraltar gave official status. The war also gave rise to an initially *ad hoc* design for a military decision-making structure involving France, Germany and the UK. This subsequently evolved into the European Security Council (ESC), which was formally established as an institution in Gibraltar for a ten-year trial period. At the same time, membership of the ESC was extended to include Italy, a medium-sized country and a small country (each chosen on a six-monthly rotating basis). With three new military operations now under its belt, the ESC has provided ample proof of its effectiveness. However, the flip side is that it has deprived the small countries of much of their influence. Also, the Gibraltar Treaty eroded the power of the Community institutions: the Commission was deprived of its exclusive right to propose new legislation and the Court of Justice lost its jurisdiction over most justice- and police-related matters. Decisions concerning Europol and management of the external borders are still taken unanimously, with no role for the Commission or Parliament in the former (the Member States ultimately refused to allow the area of police co-operation to be brought within the Community framework but closer co-operation between some of them was frequently used in the area of justice, security and home affairs). The EU's foreign-policy supremo has been criticized for being in the pocket of the three big Member States (as the Portuguese President put it recently, 'the High Representative of the Council keeps telling us how good Europe's military information technology is, but his phone only lets him call three cities: Berlin, London and Paris'). In short, the whole EU is developing a more inter-governmental approach, foreign policy is dominated by three Member States and, meanwhile, the others are waiting for things to calm down in the world outside to challenge this *de facto* triumvirate.

Unfortunately, the calm is a long time coming ... Though the Union now has a well-established reputation as the regional policeman, tension and conflict continue to erupt around its borders. The eastern parts of the continent are permanently destabilized by Russia: organized crime's hold over the leading élites continues to grow, there is ongoing conflict between central government and the regions and the economy is in a parlous state. All this has plunged the country into a worrying state of introversion, from which it emerges only sporadically to remind the world and its former satellites of the power it once had. Central Asia, the Ukraine and the Eastern European countries that have remained more or less dependent on Moscow have strayed off course along with Russia. The Union has permanent problems with its eastern border, which has become a major route in for illegal immigrants from Asia, Africa and the former Soviet Republics. The Member States that are directly affected fear that the problem may become insurmountable. This is particularly true of Poland, used as a transit corridor by Russian and Ukrainian organized crime networks despite the efforts of BordEuro and Europol to stop their activities.

Europe's southern flank is almost as worrying. In the first few years of the century, the Union neglected co-operation with the Mediterranean countries, essentially because its attention was focused on the admission of new members from Central Europe, monetary matters and internal reform. To the south, Europe has made a belated, half-hearted effort but the Euro-Mediterranean partnership never really got off the ground and the plan for a free-trade area has been postponed *sine die*. As for the eastern Mediterranean, the whole region has been destabilized by the failure of the peace process. To compensate for their lack of democratic legitimacy and serious internal problems, Turkish leaders are playing the nationalist card in their relations with their neighbours. Turkish aggressiveness, compounded by the Europeans' blatantly offhand attitude and repressive border regime, has resulted in a significant deterioration in relations between the EU and Turkey since 2005.

But Turkey does not have a monopoly on resentment against the Union. All the Mediterranean countries accuse Europe of taking advantage of the opening-up of their markets while leaving them to cope with intractable demographic, social and political problems. No government has succeeded in implementing significant economic reforms or slowing the spread of poverty; signs of instability and popular discontent are on the increase. In spite of the ill health of the region's only Islamic Republic, religious parties have become a political force to be reckoned with everywhere and could soon win power in a number of other countries – unless the generals beat them to it. Whatever ideology the governments of the region subscribe to, the situation threatens to deteriorate further under the combined effect of demographic and environmental pressures (there are reasons to fear that in ten years or so the scarcity of drinking water may lead to water wars between certain countries in the region).

It seems that Europe will have to play its new role of regional policeman for a while longer. The most recent of all the world powers, it is the one struggling against the most hostile environment, paying the price of foreign-policy inaction in the 1990s. However, the rest of the world can hardly be called a peaceful haven. The Americas have merged into a Single Market, the PAFTA (Pan-American Free Trade Area), which the US dominates with its economic and technological leverage. Washington has shifted the focus of its policy back to the American continent. The US maintains a diplomatic presence in Asia, Europe and the Middle East but now intervenes as international policeman only on its own continent, to restore order in the more unstable countries of central America or lead operations against drug and illegal-immigration cartels. The regional balance of power is less stable in Asia: China and Japan would both like to play the leading role in East Asia but neither has what it takes: diplomatic prestige *and* economic and technological prowess. Other countries, such as India, Iran and South Africa, are trying to build up their own spheres of influence with varying degrees of success. On the whole, these regional powers co-exist more or less peacefully, which is quite surprising given the weakness of the international institutions. Apart from the long-standing antagonisms between certain countries, the only real disputes revolve around trade, in particular trade between the EU and PAFTA. Lastly, there are some regions that no one has managed to stabilize, such as sub-Saharan Africa, the CIS and the Mediterranean. In all three cases Europe is on the front line.

This difficult situation on the outside is having serious repercussions on life inside the Union. People have the impression of living in a haven of fragile peace and are willing to shut their eyes to infringements of certain fundamental rights and freedoms to preserve it. Immigration policies have been tightened considerably: with the approval of the silent majority, governments have been dealing with requests for asylum in an increasingly draconian fashion and have been more vigorous in pursuing and expelling illegal immigrants. The Union's external borders are bristling with well-guarded border posts and watchtowers evoking sinister memories. The more geographically exposed Member States are beginning to look more like fortresses. Across the Union, the police and army presence has been greatly stepped up since the putting in place of the Eurovigil plan, which was introduced as a 'temporary' measure after the attacks in the winter of 2003, but has never been scaled down since. Europeans have become accustomed to the over-zealous attitude of the law-and-order authorities, which manifests itself in endless identity checks, particularly for those that stand out as immigrants. Some Member States' concern for security has prompted them to take drastic measures such as restoring the death penalty for terrorist acts and making involvement in organized-crime networks punishable by life imprisonment. In more general terms, the 'European area of freedom, security and justice' is coming to resemble a police state a little more each day. The Member States jealously guard their powers in the field of public order and are augmenting them with increasingly repressive common measures. Over the past five years, European rules on immigration, visas and asylum have steadily been tightened up to the level in the strictest Member State.

Europeans have watched their states 'get tough for law and order' without protest because they see it as an answer to the worrying situation they find themselves in. Some would like their governments to go even further. Recent opinion polls show that people feel a deep sense of unease towards the rest of the world (paraphrasing one of his predecessors, the President of Romania recently scoffed that 'the overwhelming majority of Europeans think that the EU has only one good neighbour: the Atlantic Ocean'). There is widespread intolerance towards foreigners and irritation with civil rights associations. The policy pursued in some countries of forcing immigrants to assimilate meets with tacit public approval. More generally, fear of the future and reactionary attitudes can be felt in a growing number of issues, such as minority rights and sexual equality. The European public is distinctly more narrow in its outlook and less open to change than 20 years ago.

With an electorate condoning heavy-handed policies of external and internal security, politicians have no choice but to postpone painful domestic-policy decisions, in particular reform of the welfare state. Having failed to demolish their social security systems outright, governments continue to chip quietly away at them – an approach which combines the worst of all worlds: reduced competitiveness, gradual erosion of welfare cover, rapidly increasing social exclusion and an unsatisfactory balancing act between the generations. Of course the situation is not identical in every country in the big Member States, political leaders have been bolstered by their foreign-policy operations and have on occasion been able to use their popularity to push through some difficult reforms, but across Europe social inequality is widening; and there is a general lack of support for comprehensive reform.

The lack of vitality apparent on the social front is also affecting the European economy. Sluggish economic growth is partly the result of a slow-down throughout the industrialized world: external tensions, corporate resistance to liberalization in certain industries and the rise of protectionist pressures all prevent the world from capitalizing on technological progress in the fields of information and communication. In the Union, the introduction of the euro has increased economic transparency, but governments do less than in the past to make sure the Single Market is working properly, and have no qualms about helping selected domestic companies to protect their captive markets. The stability pact has been circumvented on a number of occasions; recently some Member States even proposed that military expenditure should be excluded from public debt statistics. A number of European governments openly support breaches of competition law in high-tech industries of use to the military. In more general terms, the traditional weaknesses of the European economy persist, namely high taxation (European harmonization in this field has been postponed indefinitely) and a greater emphasis on traditional industries than our American and Asian competitors. High-tech industries, such as information technology and microelectronics, are still the poor relations in Europe's economy and it will be years before any products with civilian applications emerge from the recent military research programme in those areas. Lastly, economic and social apathy and political rigidity sustain regional inequalities. It looks as if whole chunks of the continent are doomed to spend many more years out in the wilderness.

There is also a pressing need for the countries of Europe to reform the way they are governed, as well as their economic structures and welfare systems. Recent years have seen a certain amount of backtracking: experiments with decentralisation at the end of the twentieth century did not deliver what their supporters had hoped for and the cause of open government has taken a backseat to effective government. The public are not as keen on these issues as they used to be: people's new-found trust in traditional parties and policies, in particular those with an extremist-nationalistic stance, leads them to a passive acceptance of general inefficiency and tax rises, provided they are not too obvious. After all, security policies also create a few jobs, especially for the young and unqualified, but the chaotic and arbitrary nature of public services in certain Member States is bound, sooner or later, to provoke a backlash. More generally, signs are multiplying that the European populations are experiencing a spiritual disillusion and are suffering from the collapse of the ideal of the 'open society'. The boom of alternative religious and spiritual movements clearly reveals the underlying malaise.

So the decade from 2010 to 2020 promises to be a turbulent one for Europe, on both foreign and domestic policy fronts. Some are quick to predict the decline of the Old Continent, which they think will fall behind other major regional powers. However, Europe's position relative to the United States, China, Japan or any other country, is not the main issue in any serious analysis of global trends. It is the entire international political system that is slipping back into a configuration more appropriate to the nineteenth century – at a time when the main challenges are global ones. The regional blocs now taking shape cannot hope to bring anything more than a partial solution to problems like the environment, the rise of organized crime and population growth. Unless the world's political and economic leaders rediscover the virtues of international co-operation soon, they could find themselves caught up in a vicious circle of instability, with a continuous round of famine, riots, wars over natural resources and inter-ethnic conflict that would keep them too busy even to think about finding lasting solutions. In this scenario, the Mediterranean would be the next region to follow Russia and Africa down the road to chaos. Then it would be Europe's turn, and it wouldn't stop there ...

6. What we know about the future

The scenarios take into account in an implicit fashion a number of deep-seated trends affecting Europe's present and future. For those deemed to be the most significant, the Forward Studies Unit undertook a specific analysis, the results of which are presented below. The trends differ as to the degree of certainty that can be attached to each of them. For instance, the demographic trends are 'set', in the sense that a change in the projected age structure of the European population would take at least two generations to materialize. The trend of globalization is considered fairly stable in the time frame of the scenarios, but a major politico-economic shock might alter or even reverse its course, and the weight of the different elements driving it may evolve. Other trends, like the emergence of new security threats, are of a different nature in the sense that they are mainly driven by man-made events, taking place at a precise moment in time, and can therefore be more easily influenced by political decisions.

DEMOGRAPHY (EUROPE)

Regardless of the scenario that one adopts, when it comes to demographic trends the direction of change is clearly foreseeable. Like the other parts of the industrial world, Europe is ageing. This is not an entirely new trend: the population of industrial countries has been growing older for the best part of the last 150 years, due to the decline in fertility and mortality. However, as life expectancy has risen to unprecedented high levels (as much as 80 years for women and 74 years for men born in 1990), while the number of children expected from each woman has never been so low (close to 1.5 based on 1990 data), we are approaching a situation without parallel in history: a reversal of the proportion between the young and the old. Specifically, according to the latest available projections for the EU (15 Member States):[1]

- Total population is heading toward stabilization, followed by decline after 2025[2] (increasing from its present size of around 375 million to 385 million in 2010 and to 388 million in 2020).
- The number of young persons (less than 20 years of age) is falling and will continue to do so (from around 87 million to 84 million in 2010 and to 80 million in 2020).

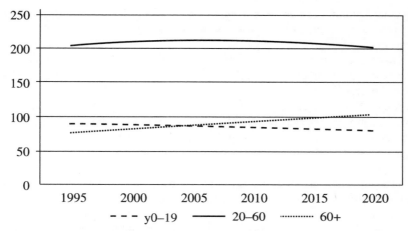

Source: Eurostat, population projections, baseline scenario.

Figure 6.1   EU population projections by age group (1995-2020) (millions)

- The number of persons aged 60 and over will continue to increase (from around 80 million to 91 million in 2010 and to 104 million in 2020). Among them, the fastest rising group will be those aged 80 and over (from around 13 million to 18 million in 2010 and to 22 million in 2020).

What will be the main consequences of this demographic shift?

One can expect that ageing populations will put increasing pressures on social programmes, essentially pension expenditure and also health care. The reduction in expenditure for education (and the possible reduction in expenditure for unemployment) will only slightly offset the increase in these two large programmes. This result is robust to different assumptions about growth and employment and takes into account the effects of the reforms already enacted that will make pension systems less generous than at present. The pressure on public budgets will be substantial, and possibly destabilizing, especially after 2010, when expenditure takes off as the baby-boom generation begins to retire.

Specifically, in the 2010-2030 period, projected expenditure increases range from 3 to 5 percentage points of GDP in several countries, compared with increases ranging from 1 to 3 percentage points in the 1995-2010 period. It is a relatively safe prediction that governments will continue to resort to 'orderly default' on their implicit pension debt (that is, rewriting pension rules to cut the benefits of the successive generations of retirees). Pressure to stem expenditure is also likely to rise in the health-care area. Options may include making patients bear a larger share of the costs, putting pressure on providers to increase cost-effectiveness, and giving new incentives to prevention.

The consequences of the demographic transition on labour markets are more difficult to predict. Given the near-stability of the working-age population, the growth of the labour force will come to depend essentially on the evolution of the activity rate.[3] This in turn will essentially revolve around the work incentives for women and older workers: currently, the activity rates for women range from over 75 per cent (the Nordic countries) to less than 50 per cent (the Mediterranean countries) and those for men aged between 55 and 59 vary from 85 per cent (Sweden) to nearly 50 per cent (Belgium). Moreover, significant gains in employment could be made in the next ten years by reducing structural unemployment from its present very high levels. It should not be assumed, however, that a declining working-age population would automatically result in the disappearance of the unemployment problem: the final equilibrium will depend on the adjustment of labour demand and wage levels. Finally, the rising proportion of prime-age and older workers in the labour force, while a potential source of productivity gains, is likely to require adaptations in existing labour market institutions, such as the link between seniority and pay, training patterns and the transition from work to retirement. If these adaptations do not occur, there is a risk that the unemployment problem will be displaced from the younger to the older section of the working population.

DEMOGRAPHY (WORLD)

The challenges posed by the demographic evolution in Europe are dwarfed by those of the world at large. World population, currently close to 6 billion, is projected to approach 6.9 billion in 2010. Nine out of every ten people added to the world population in this period will be in developing countries. As a result the demographic weight of the industrial countries, and Europe in particular, will continue to decline: by 2010, only one EU country (Germany) will be among the top 20 countries by population (Table 6.1) and the EU share of the world's population, currently at 6.3 per cent, will fall to 5.6 per cent.

Such differences in population growth are likely to result in strong migration pressures. They are reinforced by differences in the age-structure: in low-income countries over 40 per cent of the population is currently aged under 20 against less than 25 per cent in Europe. Moreover, the countries of sub-Saharan Africa and Northern Africa, which are the most likely prospective sources of immigration for Europe, are among those

Table 6.1   Top 20 countries ranked by population

	1998	2010	2020
1	China	China	China
2	India	India	India
3	United States	United States	United States
4	Indonesia	Indonesia	Indonesia
5	Brazil	Brazil	Brazil
6	Russia	Pakistan	Pakistan
7	Pakistan	Bangladesh	Nigeria
8	Japan	Nigeria	Bangladesh
9	Bangladesh	Russia	Russia
10	Nigeria	Japan	Mexico
11	Mexico	Mexico	Japan
12	Germany	Philippines	Philippines
13	Philippines	Vietnam	Vietnam
14	Vietnam	Germany	Congo (Kinshasa)
15	Egypt	Egypt	Egypt
16	Turkey	Turkey	Ethiopia
17	Iran	Iran	Iran
18	Thailand	Ethiopia	Turkey
19	United Kingdom	Congo (Kinshasa)	Germany
20	France	Thailand	Thailand

Source: US Census Bureau, International Data Base.

showing the highest fertility rates in the developing world. Excluding migratory flows, the total population of the Southern European countries of Spain, Portugal, France, Italy and Greece is estimated to remain stable at around 175 million between 1998 and 2010. By contrast, the populations of Morocco, Algeria, Tunisia, Libya and Egypt are expected to increase by 32 million in the same period, bringing their total population close to that of their European neighbours (and overtaking them in the following decades). The push factors in the over-populated developing countries are thus compounded by the pull factor of population stagnation in the more developed societies. In economic terms, migration from the former to the latter represents a welfare-enhancing, equilibrating force. However, cultural and distributional issues are likely to render the transition to a new demographic equilibrium much less smooth than purely economic considerations would suggest.

GLOBALIZATION AND INEQUALITIES

Globalization is probably the economic buzzword at the end of the twentieth century.

The basic economic facts behind the globalization debate are relatively undisputed: the steady increase in cross-border flows of trade, investment and financial capital since World War II, and the more recent acceleration as far as the two latter are concerned. A few statistics: since 1950, trade in goods has been growing at an annual rate of 6.3 per cent against 4 per cent for world production; the ratio of foreign direct investment (FDI) to GDP has risen to 21 per cent of world GDP compared to 10 per cent in 1980; daily turnover on the world financial market amounted to US$ 1500 billion in 1998, compared to 600 billion in 1989.

At the same time, if both industrial and developing countries have generally benefited from the globalization of markets (rates of growth such as those experienced by the countries of East Asia in the last 20 years would have been considered extraordinary 40 years ago), the gap between the richest and the poorest has continued to grow. In general, income per capita has been growing (slightly) faster in developing countries than in the industrial countries for the past 40 years. In the least-developed countries, however, growth rates have been consistently close to zero or even negative. The average income per capita in the G7 industrial countries was 20 times that of the seven poorest countries in 1965; it was 39 times as much in 1997.

Moreover, potentially the most threatening for social stability is the evidence of a trend toward rising income inequalities within countries, both in industrial countries and, possibly, in the world at large (Table 6.2).

The coincidence of increasing economic integration and rising income inequalities inevitably leads to the most sensitive question about globalization: will globalization exacerbate inequality? A related question is: how powerful (or powerless) are governments in the face of globalization?

To help answer this, it is worth addressing a preliminary question: what is new about globalization? Consider the following: in a number of industrial

Table 6.2   World-wide trends in income inequality (1975–95) (% of countries in terms of population)

Countries	Inequality increasing	Inequality stabilizing	Inequality decreasing	No identifiable trend
Industrial countries	71.8	1.2	27	0.0
Eastern Europe	98.1	0.0	0.0	1.9
Former USSR	100.0	0.0	0.0	0.0
Latin America	83.8	0.0	11.4	4.8
South Asia and Middle East	1.4	70.2	14.4	14.0
East Asia	79.4	4.4	16.1	0.1
Africa	31.6	11.9	7.7	48.8
World*	56.6	22.1	15.6	5.7

Note: *Sample of 77 countries representing 81.7 of the world population and 95.0 of world GDP at PPP.

Source: Calculations based on G.A. Cornia 'Globalisation and Income Distribution', paper presented at the International seminar 'Globalisation, A Challenge for Peace: Solidarity or Exclusion?' organized by the Istituto Internazionale, Jacques Maritain, Milan, 29–31 October 1998.

countries, trade flows (average of imports and exports) as a percentage of GDP are not much higher than they were before World War I and worldwide investment flows (current account surpluses/deficits) are actually still below their pre-1914 levels. Nothing new, then? The present period of globalization differs from the previous one in key respects: the importance of intra-industry (and intra-firm) trade, the emergence of an increasing number of developing countries as major exporters of manufactured products, the de-integration of production through cross-border outsourcing, the explosion of international financial markets accompanied by floating exchange rates. Last but not least, with the partial exception of the USA, cross-border labour migration is much lower than in the past.

The fragmentation of the global economy following World War I and the Great Depression suggests that de-globalization is not an impossible event, if economic and political shocks are strong enough. However, new technologies and new types of production and financial organization make it harder for governments to insulate their economies, at least on a country-by-country basis. This means that, to be effective, an anti-globalization backlash would probably have to occur in a trade-bloc form, with major regions of the world increasing barriers to the penetration of their markets. At the same time, one should not underestimate the potential of traditional and new forms of resistance to globalized markets in particular areas, such as the agro-food industry and the media, in the wake of rising concerns about the preservation of health and the environment, or cultural identity.

As to the increasing limits placed by globalization on government action, capital mobility is often said to pose the greatest threat to national autonomy, notably on monetary and tax matters. It has certainly made it more difficult for a country to fix its exchange rate: recent experience suggests that there may be little middle ground left between full exchange rate flexibility or full currency merger. The threat from international tax competition is more difficult to assess: for example, generally lower statutory tax rates on corporations in industrial countries have been accompanied by a broadening of the corporate tax base, so that the tax revenue share has generally not fallen. Yet it is at least conceivable that factor mobility, including high-skilled workers, might threaten redistribution programmes with the 'New York City syndrome' of increasing needs and a disappearing tax base. International tax co-ordination would then become a realistic option.

Freer trade and capital flows have also the potential of exacerbating income inequalities, particularly in industrial countries, where unskilled workers are put in competition with the much larger pool of labour of developing countries. The simple threat to import competing goods or to shift production abroad might suffice to force low-skilled 'Westerners' to accept pay cuts or face unemployment. There is a parallel here with the tax competition debate: experts tend to exclude the possibility that globalization has been the main cause of the recent impoverishment of the less skilled, but do not entirely rule out the possibility that international developments might dominate labour market outcomes in the future. The strongest counter-argument against this scenario of worldwide wage equalization is that ultimately all less-skilled workers in the industrial countries may be working in the non-traded sector (already only a minority sector of manufacturing). At that point trade would not affect their wages, at least in the absence of immigration from low-wage countries.

In general, experts tend to blame skill-biased technological change (that is, changes in technology continuously increasing the demand for skilled workers) rather than trade for the worsening condition of unskilled workers in industrial countries. However, there are dissenters and it is often very difficult to differentiate the effects of the two. A good example is outsourcing, that is, the decision of companies to move to low-wage countries those parts of their activities with relatively low value added in modern industry, such as assembling and other repetitive tasks. Outsourcing tends to work just like a new technology that reduces the use of unskilled workers within each industry. The debate is therefore likely to remain lively, both in scientific and political terms.

As a conclusion, one can derive the following points:

- Global economic integration has both deepened and widened over the past 50 years. The trend is likely to continue as technology overcomes existing barriers and new countries join the global market, but historical experience shows that globalization may be reversed, if the economic and political shocks are strong enough. Given current technological constraints, a hypothetical anti-globalization backlash would have to be based on trade blocs. Specific concerns about health and the environment or cultural identity may favour more concentrated forms of resistance to globalization in areas such as the agri-food industry and the media.
- Globalization is not a zero-sum game. It is an important source of economic growth as economies specialize in the sectors where they excel and align themselves to the practice of productivity leaders. However, many countries lack the minimum conditions necessary to join the global markets and their situation may continue to worsen in relative and sometimes absolute terms. Moreover, specialization requires restructuring, which can have distributional consequences. Less-skilled workers in industrial countries are a particularly vulnerable group. Such inequality-increasing effects within countries have probably been limited so far, but may become more important in the future. Free mobility of labour between poor and rich countries would reinforce trends in the same direction and therefore existing restrictions are likely to remain in place.

TECHNOLOGY AND PRODUCTIVITY

Economic growth is the central feature of modern times. Since the beginning of the nineteenth century, people have been able to observe, in the course of their lifetime, a generalized improvement in their standards of living.[4] This is likely to continue in the future. The best reason for this belief is that, since growth picked up about 200 years ago, there has been a succession of technological advances, which does not show any sign of abating. At basic level, the link between technology and growth seems pretty obvious. Putting more people to work will increase total production but not as likely on a per capita basis, as diminishing returns rapidly set in.

Moreover, new inventions allow us to do things that previously were simply impossible. Adding more and more shovels and horses would not have allowed us to reach today's level of output. Long-run growth with a static technology is simply implausible. At a deeper level, however, the link between technology and growth remains a puzzle. For example, we are often told that we live in times of unprecedented technological progress at the same time that we hear frequent complaints about the slow pace of growth of the economy. In fact, if one takes the long-term view, the latter claim is false, and the former is dubious, at least in economic terms. Take growth first. If we take a closer look at the growth performance of the major industrial countries and regions over the last 120 years, two conclusions emerge (Table 6.3):

- The 1950–73 period (appropriately named by historians the 'Golden Age') stands out as an episode of exceptionally fast growth;
- The current, post-1973 phase represents a return to normalcy. For Europe, in particular, current rates of growth still compare favourably with those recorded in previous historical periods (including the one that goes under the popular misnomer of *belle époque*).

Assessing the technological breakthroughs of the current age is more complex. Those who claim that we are going through a Third Industrial Revolution, comparable to the transformation first undergone by England 200 years ago often point to the 'explosion' of information and communication technologies (ICTs). This results in a dramatic acceleration in the ability to handle the information needed to run all kinds of economic activity. However impressive the breakthroughs in ICTs and other technologies (e.g. biotechnologies, new materials) may look, to qualify for Industrial Revolution status what matters is the impact that such technological advances have on the economy as a whole. However, economic performance to date does not show evidence of dramatic change. If the present age cannot be considered one of slow growth, it is also easy to point out that the continuing rise in R&D activity since the 1960s has gone hand in hand with a slowdown in total factor productivity, the economists' way to measure the impact of technological progress (Table 6.4).[5]

A problem is that the economic effects of technological advances can only be properly assessed much later. Experts' estimates of the contribution of computing services to future productivity growth therefore vary widely. Some experts believe that the marginal product of computing services is destined to remain relatively low, as the most productive applications have already been largely exploited. Other experts, by contrast, believe that economy-wide productivity increases of more than $^1/_2$ per cent are on the horizon, as the

Table 6.3   Long-term trends in economic growth in the USA, Europe and Japan

Country	Growth of GDP[1] (annual % change)				Growth of GDP per inhabitant (annual % change)			
	1870–1913	1913–50	1950–73	1973–92	1870–1913	1913–50	1950–73	1973–92
USA	3.9	2.8	3.9	2.4	1.8	1.6	2.4	1.4
Western Europe[2]	2.1	1.4	4.7	2.2	1.3	0.9	3.9	1.8
of which: – Germany[3]	2.8	1.1	6.0	2.3	1.6	0.3	5.0	2.1
– France	1.6	1.1	5.0	2.3	1.5	1.1	4.0	1.7
– UK	1.9	1.3	3.0	1.6	1.0	0.8	2.5	1.4
– Italy	1.9	1.5	5.6	2.7	1.3	0.8	5.0	2.4
Southern Europe[4]	1.5	1.3	6.3	3.1	1.1	0.4	4.9	1.7
Japan	2.4	2.4	9.2	3.8	1.4	0.9	8.0	3.0

Notes:
[1] GDP in 1990 dollars converted at purchasing power parities.
[2] Austria, Belgium, Denmark, Finland, France, West Germany, Italy, the Netherlands, Norway, Sweden, Switzerland, UK.
[3] West Germany after 1950.
[4] Greece, Ireland, Portugal. Spain.

Source: Calculations based on A. Maddison, *L'Economie Mondiale 1820–1992. Analyse et Statistiques. OECD,* Paris, 1995.

European futures

Table 6.4   R&D effort and economic growth

	R&D expenditure (% of GDP)			Total factor productivity[1] (% change per year)		
Country	1965	1970–79	1980–89	1990–94	1960–73	1973–79	1979–93
USA	2.76	2.36	2.70	2.76	1.6	–0.4	0.4
Japan	1.55	1.97	2.63	3.02	5.6	1.3	1.4
Germany	1.60	2.18	2.67	2.59	2.6	1.8	1.0
France	2.03	1.79	2.15	2.41	3.7	1.6	1.2
UK	2.30	2.15	2.25	2.19	2.6	0.6	1.4
Italy	n.a.	0.80	1.04	1.29	4.4	2.0	1.0

Note: [1] TFP growth is equal to a weighted average of the growth in labour and capital productivity. The sample period averages for capital and labour shares are used as weights.

Source: *OECD*, 'OECD Economies at a Glance. Structural Indicators', Paris, 1996.

productive potential of ICIs is finally realized, not least thanks to an apprenticeship process by workers and consumers alike. Somewhere in between are those who stress the great potential but also the peculiar obstacles that characterize the new technologies. They point out that the institutional framework that has accompanied the development of the industrial society is no longer suited to supporting an apprenticeship process and transactions that increasingly revolve around the exchange of knowledge. Finally, especially in the case of some technologies (e.g. biotechnologies), one should not underestimate the possibility of an explicit rejection on cultural grounds, linked to the dangers that these might conceivably pose to the very basis of life.

As a conclusion, one can stress the following points:

- Productivity growth is currently in line with its long-run historical trends, which may suggest that we are not in for significant accelerations or slowdowns;
- Technology holds the key to productivity increases, but inventing new technology is less important than using it effectively. Given the time lag that separates invention from exploitation, the big question about the next 15–20 years really concerns the ability to exploit technologies that already exist. This ability in turn is linked to social institutions and cultural attitudes, with which technologies interact.

SOCIETAL TRENDS AND VALUES

During the twentieth century, many ot the traditional features of the European societies changed. The two world wars that shook the continent did not only result in the death of millions of people and a revision of the balance of power among European states, but also brought about a change in national boundaries, the dislocation of millions of people and the creation of new political systems (democracies in the West and communist totalitarian states in the East). The post-World War II period spelled a new era in Western Europe characterized by political stability, unprecedented economic growth, mass consumerism and evolving modern welfare states. Gradually, new values and perceptions emerged which are often associated both with economic and social modernization and with democratic emancipation.

Today, we witness a number of deep socio-economic trends that are influencing Western European societies in a similar fashion. These trends are intrinsically linked to new social behaviours and societal values. Sometimes this transition has been described in terms of a paradigm shift according to which our contemporary societies are leaving the modern (industrial) form of organization and production to take on distinctive post-modern traits. Leaving the polemic on the dominant direction of the post-modern society aside, the countries in Western Europe have undergone a number of changes in the last 40-odd years in features such as the material well-being of individuals, family structure and education.

In the socio-economic field the most striking feature is a general rise in the standard of living which has been accompanied by ever-more sophisticated social security systems. Improved material well-being has been translated into better housing and household equipment and in a general improvement in public health (contributing to the phenomenon of ageing). In the last decades of the twentieth century the economy has undergone profound structural changes which can be observed, for instance, in the expansion of the service sector, especially in terms of employment. Another distinctive, and related, socio-economic change is the increasing number of women in the labour market.

In Europe, there has been a marked change in the household composition away from the extended family and towards the nuclear family, typically composed of parents and one or two children. However, in many Western European countries, the nuclear family is in decline. In fact, in the Nordic countries and Germany, one-person households now account for more than one-third of the total.[6] Other household types on the increase are lone-parent households and couples without children. The reasons for the changing household composition vary, but one obvious factor is the ageing of the population (in Finland, for example, 80 per cent of all women aged 75 years and over live alone). The phenomenon can also partly be explained by other generalized demographic and social behaviours such as the decline in birth rates, the fall in the number of marriages and the rise in the rate of divorce. The household composition is of course much more than a statistical measurement, as it reflects social behaviour and practices. To make the picture livelier, we could add some national characteristics. For instance, almost two-thirds of all children in Sweden and Denmark are born outside marriage, while in Italy and Greece the proportion is under 10 per cent. The UK has the highest rate of lone-parent households, followed by Sweden and Denmark. The social habit of cohabitation is becoming increasingly frequent in the Nordic countries and in some other European countries, while it is more rare in southern Europe. In the southern European countries, multigenerational households remain quite common, as one-fifth of the population still live in this way.

Finally, the general rise in the years spent in schooling and training in Europe is mentioned here as a third socio-economic trend. Today schooling starts earlier and finishes later in life, and the level of educational attainment has risen both in terms of upper secondary and tertiary education. Western European states with an initial lower level of attainment have made the most significant advances. For instance, the proportion of those aged between 25 and 29 in Greece, Spain, Italy and Portugal having completed at least upper secondary education is at least twice that of their compatriots aged between 50 and 59. In terms of gender, there are now roughly as many women enrolled in secondary and tertiary education as men. Where social inequalities still persist, they are more likely to be linked to the socio-economic situation of the family or the educational level of the parents. Lifelong learning has not yet achieved its stated aims in the sense that continued vocational training is still benefiting young and already highly qualified employees at the expense of 'older' workers and those with low initial education. In some Western European countries (the UK, Denmark and Sweden), tertiary education has become increasingly accessible to the adult population as can be seen from the increasing number of new university entrants over 30 years of age.

A value-change has accompanied European socio-economic development, pointing towards a notable decline in traditional values and a strengthening of 'universal individualism'. This change is translated into a decline in the respect for, and even rejection of, different forms of established authority (political, administrative and social), followed by a refusal to subordinate the individual to the group and accompanied by the diminishing prestige of science, technology and rationality. Universal individualism should not be understood as a form of pure personal egoism, but as a stronger emphasis on the individual's freedom of choice and equal rights between human beings.

Roughly summarized, the value-change has taken the following form in four broad areas (based on the European Values Studies of 1981 and 1990):

- The family is still the most important area in life before work, friends or leisure. The traditional family concept (the nuclear family) is changing to include new alternative ways of living together (see above). Accompanying this trend is a change of attitudes making Europeans more tolerant towards non-traditional behaviour. Therefore, social practices beyond the traditional family, such as living together and having children without being married, or homosexuality, are becoming increasingly accepted. In terms of tolerance towards non-traditional behaviour, there has long been a gap between Southern and Northern Europe, with the latter being more permissive in its attitudes and practices. However, the young in Southern Europe tend to express opinions regarding alternative social practices that are considerably more advanced than their older compatriots.
- Work is of course still intimately connected with the ability of individuals to earn their livelihood and improve their socio-economic standard. The importance of work, however, goes increasingly beyond the mere earning of one's living. Work is now more than ever before linked to personal self-fulfilment and to one's image of oneself. It is also an important source of social integration. New economic structures and working practices are, however, eroding the link between work and the identification with a specific social class.
- Socio-economic advancement (e.g. improved levels of education, standard of living) and changing societal values (e.g. individualism, declining allegiance to hierarchy) are having a profound impact on Europeans' attitudes towards the traditional features of representative democracy. For instance, the rate of participation in general elections is decreasing, as is membership of political parties. Europeans are not becoming less interested in politics as such, but they are seeking more active and participatory forms of political expression. Established ideologies and their representatives (political parties) are increasingly felt as a hindrance to the free expression of personal opinions on society's direction. Alongside traditional political movements, new organized players have emerged. They have often grown up as one-issue (protest) movements against, for instance, environmental degradation or nuclear armament. Lately, a dense web of non-governmental organizations has emerged. Their activities extend to cover several diverse areas, and they are perceived by some as reflecting more accurately the interests of Europeans than established political parties or traditional interest groups do. The concept of civil society is gaining

currency. Another trend, clearly noticeable in the past years, is the emergence of one-issue parties, be it the organized version of popular movements (e.g. Greens) or groups driven by popular mistrust of established political parties and the workings of political systems. These political movements, both to the right and left of the traditional political spectrum, have succeeded in attracting popular support because of the widespread disillusionment with traditional politics – and they tend to have an impact upon established political parties.

- The declining social status of religion as an organizing element of society is partly due to the fragmentation of society (urbanization, erosion of class structures, professional groups or regional communities). It also derives from the questioning of traditionally defined authority. It is important to point out, however, that although the number of practising Christians is declining, this should not be interpreted as people becoming less religious, but rather that they are seeking alternative forms to express their beliefs. In fact, Europeans are putting an increased emphasis on the individual's spiritual experience at the expense of traditional religious structures – as witnessed by the spread of religious sects and increased interest for non-Western cults.

It is important to point out that these are generalized trends, which should be treated with caution in respect to individual European societies. Historical experience, symbols and traditions are important in shaping the particular way in which a society adapts to socio-economic change. Equally, the level of socio-economic advancement and the number of years of functioning democracy play an important role for the spread and acceptance of new values and the emergence of new social practices. In conclusion, two final remarks should be added. First, in terms of adherence to post-modern values and acceptance of change, the generational factor is decisive: each generation is systematically more advanced in terms of attitudes and social values than the previous one. Second, at a time when profound changes are taking place, sometimes to the bewilderment of the individual citizens, the same citizens seem to be increasingly at ease with multiple belongings (geographic, social, civic and religious).

NEW SECURITY THREATS

The end of the Cold War did not, as many hoped at the end of the 1980s, spell the end of armed conflict in Europe. It did, however, dramatically change the strategic landscape of the continent and beyond, and with it the nature and origin of security threats. In the 1990s, threats became increasingly associated with non-military phenomena of a complex kind. The nature of military conflicts changed: organized wars between states for power and sovereignty became rare, while intra-state and often ethnically defined conflicts of legitimacy took the place. For instance, in 1997, of the 25 major conflicts recorded, only one, between India and Pakistan, was of an interstate nature, and all the others were internal conflicts. This trend is reinforced by the growing number of internationally recognized states: there were 44 states in 1850, 60 in 1938, 144 in 1983 and as many as 191 in 1995. In many ways, this phenomenon may seem to conflict with the contemporary trends of globalization and regional integration (e.g. the EU). However, it can also be seen as the result of the prevailing structure of international relations, which induces ethnic groups to strive towards greater self-determination in order to win international recognition for their claims, and leaves them *de facto* battling for political autonomy and independence. In the process, we witness the creation of small, often ethnically defined, states (South Eastern Europe, Africa, Asia, etc.), whose capacity for economic and political survival is not guaranteed. It is something of a paradox that the proliferation of small states and the nation-building process taking place within newly independent states go hand in hand with the progressive weakening of the 'old' nation-states in the Western world.

The end of communist dominance in Eastern Europe opened the perspective of a united, peaceful continent. In this respect, the experience of more than 40 years of economic and political integration, making war unthinkable between Western European states, has acted as an important factor for stabilization in Central and Eastern Europe. The prospect of membership of the EU, and of other Western organizations, has had a beneficial effect on the candidate countries in this part of Europe by imposing a policy of democratization and good-neighbourliness.

The end of the Cold War also brought into the open some phenomena that the totalitarian communist system had kept the lid on. The newly democratized states found themselves in the awkward position of, on the one hand, supporting the emergence of national identity as a means of nation-building and, on the other, coping with claims from ethnic minorities for economic and political rights. In some cases these claims were perceived as a threat to the stability of the new state. A complex ethnic composition, along with a mismatch between state and nation in some cases, fuelled the rise of nationalist politics in Eastern Europe. Intra-state as well as inter-state tension rose as a result, with the war in former Yugoslavia as the most extreme example. The (peaceful) separation of Czechoslovakia, tensions surrounding Hungarian minorities in neighbouring countries and the war of words concerning the Baltic Russians in Estonia and Latvia are other, less dramatic, examples. In the past years, ethnically related tension has been significantly reduced as many countries in Central and Eastern Europe have systematically adopted measures to improve the socio-economic and political conditions of national minority groups.

The end of the Cold War and the opportunities offered by globalization in terms of international finance, communication and easier travel, have all contributed to the emergence of phenomena threatening the stability of Europe. These new risks, bundled together under the soft security umbrella (as opposed to hard security, i.e. outright war), include organized crime, trafficking in human beings, terrorism, techno-crime, illegal drugs-dealing, trafficking in arms and other harmful substances (nuclear waste, etc.). These phenomena are not new in themselves. What is new is their intensity, their increasingly international character, their ready use of new technologies and communication and their heightened interconnection. Today, terrorist groups having lost their main sponsors are less 'ideologically correct', and do not refrain from earning their living from drugs-dealing or other illegal activities. Similarly, criminals take advantage of the opportunities offered by illegal drugs-dealing, smuggling, and trafficking in human beings, only to launder the proceeds in international financial markets or through portfolio investment in emerging markets. Organized criminality has become truly international in its ability to diversify into new geographical areas and its skill in establishing co-operation networks between different national groupings.

The effects of these new security threats have hit societies both in Western and Eastern Europe. However, the new democracies in the East are probably more vulnerable to attempts of organized criminal groupings to influence or in extreme cases (e.g. Albania) control political power, or quite simply to take a stake in the economic activities of a given country through investment in privatized companies.

There is also a risk that the countries of Central and Eastern Europe will have a harder time in coping with the effects on their societies of drug abuse, inflows of illegal immigrants and crime because of inadequate financial resources, lack of sophisticated equipment and the operational immaturity of newly reformed institutions such as the police, security forces, border guards or the judicial system. However, infiltration and corruption of the state and its institutions by criminal organizations are serious threats to all European countries and the rule of law must be underpinned by active means. Therefore, the new security risks that are already making themselves felt all over Europe constitute a classical case of a multidimensional problem that can only be confronted by a concerted approach from a variety of actors. Viable solutions are dependent on the pooling of national resources at the European and international levels, and on the capacity of state actors to overcome the limits imposed by their national judicial systems and the lack of practical experience of close institutionalized co-operation in areas considered as intimately linked to national sovereignty.

ENVIRONMENT

Trends in population and economic activity condition the size of the environment problem. Environmental stresses reflect an imbalance between what people consume and what natural systems can provide. If consumption is taken as the general source of pressure on the environment, imbalances in consumption matter as much as population imbalances, or even more, in dealing with the environmental problem. This point can be neatly illustrated by adjusting population figures to reflect an equivalent amount of consumption: in terms of consumption-adjusted population, the USA exceeds the sum of the two most populous countries in the world, China and India, by as much as 70 per cent (Table 6.5).

There is however no single measure of environmental stress, and the effects of economic activity on the environment are by no means uniform. On the contrary they vary, depending on the environmental dimension considered, the level of development reached and, last but not least, the policy choices adopted.

Specific examples may illustrate the complex relationship between environmental degradation and economic activity. For some pollutants (e.g. suspended particles in urban air), conditions improve steadily with higher per capita income and the associated rises in living standards. For other pollutants (e.g. several forms of air and water contamination), there appears to be an inverted-u-shaped relationship with output: environmental quality deteriorates in the early stages of economic growth until a turning point is reached beyond which higher income is associated with lower pollution. Finally, for some types of pollution (e.g. carbon dioxide – CO_2 – and nitrous oxides), there is no evidence that a turning point has yet been reached.

Some environmental issues are extremely localized and location specific (e.g. urban air pollution). Others, by contrast, are the typical example of global problems, in which stress inflicted in one part of the world could have serious consequences everywhere (e.g. global warming). In reviewing the main

Table 6.5   Consumption-adjusted population (1990)

Country	Population	Adjusted population
China	1139	9329
India	853	3907
United States	249	22 993

Source: Commission of Global Governance, *Our Global Neighbourhood*, Oxford University Press.

dimensions of the environmental issue, it is worth concentrating on such external effects, because it is there that Europe, being a high-income, stagnant-population area less threatened by its local pollution problems,[7] faces the most intractable dilemmas and possibly the most serious threats. In general, the environmental issue, like the issue of migration, is where a new form of interdependence is emerging 'vulnerability interdependence', which can link areas of the world irrespective of their degree of economic integration.

What follows is a brief review of the main areas of environmental stress, concentrating on the implications for the world at large and the possible repercussions on Europe.

With growth and development there is a tendency for forest land to be converted to cultivation and pasture and then to urban land. About one third of the land area of the earth supports very limited biological activity (cities, deserts), one third is land for cultivation and pasture and one third is forest and savannah. The declining proportion of cultivated land and pasture is a serious problem in many developing countries, but the even faster disappearance of tropical forest (especially in Latin America, which accounts for almost 60 per cent of this) raises a potential threat to mankind's future on at least two counts: the aggravation of the greenhouse effect due to higher emission and lower absorption of carbon dioxide (CO_2) (see below) and the decline in genetic diversity resulting from the extinction of plant and animal species. Some 40 per cent of medical prescriptions are either based on or synthesized from natural compounds. Yet less than 10 per cent of known plant species and a small fraction of known invertebrates (themselves a small proportion of the unknown total) have been examined for their possible medicinal value. This is just one reason why a man-made 'extinction spasm' could ultimately backfire on the human species.

Agricultural and economic development affects, and is affected by, the quantity and quality of water supplies. In most countries agriculture represents by far the largest share of freshwater withdrawals (60–80 per cent and as much as 90 per cent in some countries). Scarcity of water resources raises concern for long-term development prospects in some regions (North Africa, Central Asia and the Middle East). Where supplies are shared by more than one state, increasing scarcity is likely to become an important source of conflict.

Economic growth has a direct and positive effect on energy consumption. This relationship breaks down only at the highest income levels, where per capita energy consumption can stabilize or even decrease in connection with increasing productivity.[8] In turn, energy consumption has important environmental consequences. A major by-product of energy consumption is emission of CO_2, biggest of 'the greenhouse gases'. Scientists predict that, if the present growth rate of CO_2 emission continues, this may lead to significant rises in the earth's average temperature (global warming). Possible consequences of global warming include rising sea levels, reduced water flows, depleted agriculture, increased health hazards (skin cancer), urban smog and increased weather instability. Estimates vary widely, however, as to the extent, timing and distribution of these consequences. Most estimates suggest that significant consequences will materialize during the first half of the twenty-first century and developing countries will be most vulnerable. Yet some studies suggest the possibility of dramatic climactic events as early as 2010: according to one scenario, a drastic flip in oceanic circulation would affect the Gulf Stream current, leading to a large climate change, with immediate impact on living conditions in Northern European countries. Even if the areas that will be worst affected by global warming are located outside Europe, the resulting economic and social strains are unlikely to be contained. Already environmental change has been identified as a possible destabilization, which can ultimately degenerate into armed conflict. High-income countries (by and large, the US, the EU and Japan) account for almost half of the present level CO_2 emissions, but the growth is concentrated in the developing countries, with China and India already accounting for almost one sixth of the total.

Global warming is a typical example of an environmental problem requiring action on a global scale. The UN Convention on Climate Change represents the beginning of such a policy. Even assuming that the international engagements will be fulfilled,[9] the prevention of global warming is likely to require much deeper cuts in emissions, with the issue of burden-sharing between the industrial countries and the developing countries coming inevitably to the fore.

NOTES

1. Eurostat baseline projection, assuming an improvement in life expectancy of around three years on present levels, a small increase in fertility (still below 2 children per woman in 2025) and immigration of about 500,000 persons per year.
2. The EU-15 population is expected to peak at around 390 in 2025 and begin to decline thereafter.
3. The activity rate is defined as the proportion of those working or actively seeking work in the working-age population (15–64 years of age).
4. To assess the standard of living of a country, other factors have to be taken into account besides productivity. For example, the 'human development index' calculated by the United Nations Development Program combines several indicators, including life expectancy at birth and education. Furthermore, productivity-based measures of standard of living neglect at least two large areas affecting the quality of life: non-market activities, including the services of domestic work and the value of leisure; the variation in the availability of natural and environmental resources and the services provided. There is no commonly accepted methodology for taking into account these factors in measuring welfare across countries and time. Existing attempts point to a long-run improvement but give conflicting indications on the prevailing trends since the 1970s.

5. Total factor productivity is the measure of the efficiency with which capital and labour are employed in the economy.
6. All data in this and following paragraphs are from *Social portrait of Europe*, Eurostat, 1998.
7. This does not mean that Europe does not face serious environmental problems of its own, not all of localized nature. For example, millions of consumer, agricultural and industrial products and processes result in the release of persistent organic (carbon-based) pollutants and toxic metals. These can disperse over long distances and tend to accumulate in groundwater and soil, with potentially dangerous effects on the food chain and human health.
8. For example, per capita energy consumption in Germany has declined from 4600 kg oil-equivalent in 1980 to 4100 kg in 1994.
9. Under the obligations of the Kyoto Protocol, the EU is to cut greenhouse gas emissions by 8%, the United States by 7% and Japan by 6% between 2008 and 2012.

7. The scenarios at a glance (key drivers)

This section presents a selection of variables that were considered in writing each of the scenarios (see also the section on methodology, *How We Built the Scenarios*). For each variable a succinct description is provided, characterizing its behaviour in a given scenario. Because they interrelate across the different scenarios, the variables receive the name of 'key drivers'. To capture the interrelations, the scenarios and the key drivers are presented in a matrix format (Figure 7.1). Read vertically, the matrix describes the scenarios through the key drivers; read horizontally, it describes the key drivers through the scenarios. The horizontal reading is particularly interesting, as it allows the reader to appreciate the similarities and the dissimilarities across the scenarios on a number of important points. For this reason, the analysis follows the horizontal reading, highlighting how the key drivers behave in the different scenarios.

TECHNOLOGY/WORK ORGANIZATION

Two scenarios, *Triumphant Markets* and *Shared Responsibilities*, are characterized by trend acceleration in productivity growth as new technologies, especially in the field of information and communication, realize their potential in full. The two scenarios differ fundamentally, however, as to the hypothesis underlying the successful exploitation of the new technologies. In *Triumphant Markets*, this occurs through the unleashing of the forces of competition, whereas the guiding idea of *Shared Responsibilities* is that the new technologies will fulfil their promise only if a process of social apprenticeship is properly encouraged. The other scenarios are characterized by a slight slowdown of growth, which is broadly consistent with the performance of the European economy in the last two decades and the expected effects of demographic evolution. The slowdown is more accentuated in *Turbulent Neighbourhoods*, which is characterized by armed conflict and rising protectionism, and, at least in an initial phase, in *Creative Societies*.

SCENARIO	Triumphant Markets	the Hundred Flowers	Shared Responsibilities	Creative Societies	Turbulent Neighbourhoods
KEY DRIVERS					
Technology/work organization	'Third Industrial Revolution' accompanied by explosion of entrepreneurship ('virtual enterprise'). Unchallenged leadership of the American model in technological innovation and enterprise organization (shareholder value).	Trend growth slowdown. Exploitation of some technologies – e.g. bio-technologies – restrained by popular opposition. Devolution of large organizations, explosion of (tele-) one-person operations and informal networks.	'Third Industrial Revolution' facilitated by policies for re-orientation of technologies toward the users (public/ private partnerships). Stakeholder model of enterprise. 'win-win' flexibility.	Trend growth slowdown. Strong political impulsion to develop green technologies and training technologies. Private investment in certain technologies – e.g. bio-technologies – discouraged. Re-organization of enterprises around democratic/egalitarian imperative.	Accentuated trend growth slowdown. Europe increasingly at disadvantage in world competition, especially in hi-tech sectors. Political interference in re-organization of large enterprises.
Culture/values	Strong emphasis on self-reliance. Widespread feeling of insecurity. Residual family solidarity. Materialism and consumerism. Demonization of 'idleness' and acceptance of social exclusion.	Belief in neighbourhood solidarity and local self-help: women particularly active. Paid work less important. Anti-consumerism and do-it-yourself, but enthusiasm for information and communication technologies. 'Green' values.	Renaissance of social/ ecological awareness. Belief in responsibility and civic solidarity. Widespread tolerance of diversity. Some 'political correctness'.	Revolutionary social/ ecological awareness. Reaction against structures dominated by 'economic rationality'. Encouragement of popular creativity.	Increasing risk-aversion. Fear of the future. 'Back to roots' intolerance (including gender backlash). Creeping racism. Concern with economic and even physical security (urban crime, mafias, war in the near abroad).
Governance: • politics	New political elite vs. bureaucracy and trade unions. Regions vs. central governments (national and EU). 'Inequality of governance' across localities and social groups. Importance of lobbies and private media. 'Law and order' politics.	Regions and localities vs. central government (new Middle Age of city-states). Crisis of large bureaucracies and nation-states. Creation of new states.	New politicians vs. old bureaucrats. European initiative for reform of public sector (2001): subsidiarity at all levels (charters regulating relations between EU–Member States, Member States–regions).	Violent uprisings (in a number of countries) sparkled by EU co-ordinated plan to cut social protection. Europe-wide forums (Agoras) to discuss future of European societies. Crisis and reform of nation-states around socio-ecological priorities.	(Large) nation-states exploiting threat to security to reassert government authority. 'Law and order' politics. Shift of political centre of gravity towards right-wing populism ('Fortress Europe'). Re-legitimization of the state.
• general public	People withdrawing from public life. Mistrust of collective action. Success of single-issue NGOs.	Participation at local level, apathy at national and European level (especially large states). Mistrust of government and big business (including media): disobedience, tax evasion, boycotts, abstention.	Important minority of 'active citizens' conditioning political and community life. Broad consensus for reform of public sector and social institutions.	Increasing participation in community and political life following a period of social upheaval. Importance of 'social entrepreneurs' networked across Europe.	Political passivity and diffuse support of authoritarianism. Media encouraging fear of diversity.

SCENARIO	Triumphant Markets	the Hundred Flowers	Shared Responsibilities	Creative Societies	Turbulent Neighbourhoods
KEY DRIVERS					
• administration	Downsizing of public sector. Outsourcing of public services. Private sector taking over traditional public functions.	National administrations largely incapable of reform. Increasing irrelevance of bureaucracies. Public functions performed by associations and private organizations.	Reform of public sector according to the principles of decentralization, transparency, responsibility, subsidiarity. Increased role of evaluation and control mechanisms relative to regulation and implementation (shrinking of traditional ministries).	Interpenetration of public and private non-profit sector non-governmental organizations active in the provision of public services (education, training, assistance to low-income people).	Rollback of public sector reform. Security prevailing over transparency. Centralism discouraging flexibilization. Obsolescence of public services.
EU institutions	Minimal institutional reform. Weakening of common policies: nationalization of CAP, deep cuts in Structural Funds, 'EEA-ization' of EU. Commission reduced to Single Market authority. Limited intergovernmental police co-operation. Enlargement to 10 CEECs, Cyprus and Malta (2005–2008), EFTA countries (2004) and Turkey (after 2007).	No institutional reform (Commissioners numbers increasing). Weakening of common policies (CAP downsized) in the absence of stable budgetary framework. Trend toward semi-detached membership or even withdrawal (resistance of rich regions). Enlargement to 4 CEECs (2006), further enlargement frozen.	Initial limited reform of institutions. Enlargement to 10 CEECs, Cyprus and EFTA (2004–2009). Further reform of institutions (after 2005): strengthening of new common policies (foreign and security policy, justice and home affairs); decentralization in implementation, increase of EU budget, Council reformed on 'collegia' principle, ESC replaced by 'European popular juries'.	Limited institutional reform. Enlargement to 5 CEECs, Cyprus and Malta (2008), further enlargement dragging on. Strong development of social and environmental policies. Common policies on justice and home affairs.	Initial limited reform of institutions. Further reform after 'Thirst Wars' (2003–2004): European Security Council (D, F, I., UK, plus 2 other Member States on rotation); common border police (Bordeuro) and intelligence services (Eurosec); reduction of powers of the Commission and the European Court of Justice. Intergovernmental approach. Enlargement to 5 CEECs. Further enlargement dragging on.
Labour market and social policies	Deregulation and individualization of industrial relations. Terminal decline of trade unions. Downsizing of safety nets (generalized means-testing) and privatization of social services (expansion of private pensions, private health care).	Managed flexibility in some countries ('competitive corporatism'), informal flexibility in other countries ('implicit disentitlement'). General increase of moonlighting and 'grey sector'. Diffusion of barter and skill exchanges (especially in marginal sectors).	'Competitive corporatism': trade unions reaching out to non-core workers (and non-workers); employers renouncing individualization of industrial relations; governments implementing labour market and welfare reform (employment subsidies, individual social insurance accounts). Local confidence and employment pacts.	'Green corporatism' with important role for non-profit sector. Labour market and welfare state reform: limited flexibilization of labour market regulations (especially in the public sector); principle of 'flexible biographies' with credits accumulated also in social economy and childcare; extension of voucher system also to promote consumption of culture.	Incomplete reform of labour market and welfare state. Uneven deregulation and dual labour markets: insiders vs. outsiders. Increasing privatization of social services for the well-off. Further tightening of immigration policies coupled with forced assimilation measures.

SCENARIO	Triumphant Markets	the Hundred Flowers	Shared Responsibilities	Creative Societies	Turbulent Neighbourhoods
KEY DRIVERS					
Other economic policies	Tax and expenditure reduction. EMU working without need of enhanced policy co-ordination. Project of worldwide exchange rate arrangement. Reduced industrial policies targeted at SMEs and R&D.	Minimum of macroeconomic stability maintained but economic policies diminished by lack of compliance. Minimal EU policy co-ordination and non-extension of EMU to new Member States. Public investment neglected. Single Market hampered by non-enforcement.	EMU working in the framework of enhanced policy co-ordination: EU cyclical stabilization mechanism; EU rules for taxation of mobile factors. Increased co-ordination of education and R&D policies targeted at learning information and communications technologies.	Political uprisings disturbing EMU working (deep recession, budgetary instability, capital flight). Subsequent consolidation of EMU with introduction of cyclical stabilization mechanism. Increased political accountability of ECB. EU financial protectionism. 'Green' reform of national accounts. Labour-friendly, environment-friendly taxation. Strong incentives for the social economy.	Economic policies conditioned by security concerns (military expenditure, protection of sensitive industries). EMU working under close political supervision: ECB's independence diminished; circumvention of Stability Pact; non-extension of EMU to new Member States. Single Market hampered re-assertion of national industrial polices.
Globalization	Steadily increasing freedom of trade and investments (growing importance of intangibles). Complete removal of trade barriers (including non-tariff equivalents) envisaged for 2025 (Planet Round). Insufficient attention to non-economic issues (crime, environment). Increasing inequality.	Inertial advance of globalization. Decoupling between technology-driven globalization and multilateral co-operation. Self-regulation prevailing in economic areas, risk of chaos in other areas (crime, environment). NGOs mushrooming in global governance void.	Globalization/regionalization advancing. EU-led attempts at greater international co-ordination in economic and non-economic areas (development, crime, environment). Emerging global civil society increasingly integrated into international institutions.	Politically induced slowdown in globalization. Anti-multinationals backlash (especially in Europe). EU practising 'social' and 'green' protectionism. NGOs key to inter-regional political consensus.	Slowdown in globalization. World trade and politics increasingly organized around regional blocs. Neglect of gaps in world economic order (especially international finance and development).
Regional security	Free-trade and market integration bind the continent together. Lack of determined policies to deal with rising insecurity becomes a problem after 2010.	Fragmentation and erosion of established structures permit spread of organized crime and ethnic tension. Local outbreaks of violence.	Enlargement accompanied by a forceful neighbourhood policy based on 'partnerships' with neighbouring countries. Regional security improved.	Inward-looking during revolutionary period, the EU is faced with regional insecurity. No consistent strategy since pressure to deal with environmental and social problems is coupled with restricted border policy.	Initial disregard for mounting security problems around the EU, forces the Member States to take muscular military action to restore peace.

SCENARIO	Triumphant Markets	the Hundred Flowers	Shared Responsibilities	Creative Societies	Turbulent Neighbourhoods
KEY DRIVERS					
Central and Eastern Europe	'Fast and loose' enlargement poses problem of the non-respect of rules. Some countries emerging as 'economic tigers'. Absence of major conflicts and lack of EU security policy. Threat of organized crime.	Enlargement blocked at half-way point aggravating political and economic instability. Stranglehold of organized crime and threat of ethnic/ecological conflicts. Insufficient European neighbourhood policies (conflicting interests of D and F).	Gradual enlargement accompanied by robust neighbourhood policies. Development of pan-European security umbrella addressing soft-security concerns. Positive socio-economic development in the region.	CEECs alienated by 'red-green' revolution in Western Europe. Little understanding of EU socio-environmental priorities. Lack of neighbourhood policy.	'Thirst Wars'. Heavy EU inflitary intervention led by big member states. Persisting instability beyond EU borders. Chaos engulfing part of Eastern Europe. Major problems with organized crime, terrorism and immigration.
Mediterranean	Mediterranean free trade area. Economic growth only partially offsetting demographic and environmental problems.	Worsening economic/social situation. Authoritarian regimes and Islamic uprising. Lack of EU neighbourhood policies (conflicting interests of D and F). Environmental degradation overlooked.	Gradually improving economic/social situation. Strengthening of economic and political EU/Med co-operation (OCOMED). Democratization making progress.	Worsening economic/social situation. Authoritarian regimes and Islamic uprising. Lack of EU neighbourhood policies. Migratory pressures on the EU are rising quickly.	Risk of political and social explosion. Vicious spiral of Islamic terrorism and military repression. Aborted attempt at EU/Med partnership. Closed frontiers and rising migratory pressure lead to high illegal immigration into the EU from the region.
USA	Superior economic performance and un-challenged global leadership. Continuing pivot of (NATO-centred) network of alliances but diminishing requirement for military intervention.	Economic performance according to historic trends. Reduced politico-military involvement and diminishing economic interest in Europe. Selective approach to global issues: privileged relationship with China and Latin America.	Continuing economic dynamism. Less political involvement and occasional clashes with (more assertive) Europe. Multilateral approach to international relations slowly gaining ground.	Economic performance according to historic trends. Increasing internal opposition to globalization. Concentration on domestic problems and decreasing engagement in rest of the world. Tensions with EU on international regimes (trade, finance, environment). Privileged relationship with Latin America and Asia.	Economic performance below historic trends. Mounting isolationism Concentration on the Americas (Pan-American Free Trade area). Military withdrawal from Europe.
Russia	Gradual political stabilization and economic recovery. Reinforced bilateral relationship with USA (agreed 'OSCEization' of NATO). Stronger relations with China and NIS.	Muddling through and inward-looking attitude. Increasing strength of regions. Estrangement and tension with EU. Reinforced bilateral relationship with USA.	Political stabilization and economic recovery. Reinforced bilateral relationship with EU (EU-Russia free trade agreement).	Persistent politico-economic confusion. Estrangement with inward-looking EU.	Increasing political and economic disintegration. Stranglehold of organized crime. Involvement in regional conflicts.

SCENARIO	Triumphant Markets	the Hundred Flowers	Shared Responsibilities	Creative Societies	Turbulent Neighbourhoods
KEY DRIVERS					
Asia	Successful economic transition along free-market lines. Economic growth in China resulting in increasing regional inequalities and weakening of central power. Erosion of economic supremacy and weak regional role of Japan.	Uneven economic transition. Increased differentiation in Southeast Asia's performance. China evolving into loose federation with increasing regional discrepancies. Weakening of economic and political role of Japan.	Successful economic transition but some inward re-centring. Strengthening of regional organizations around Chinese leadership. China increasingly involved in global co-operation. Economic recovery in Japan (ambitious in-depth reform) but persistently weak political role.	Difficult economic transition (world recession). Persistent crisis in Japan leading to a partial embrace of European 'red-green' revolution. Economic difficulties frustrating China's world power ambitions.	Difficult economic transition (world economic slowdown and increasing protectionism). China–Japan rivalry. Regional conflicts.

Figure 7.1 Scenarios at a glance

CULTURE/VALUES

Self-reliance and economic achievement are the key values permeating *Triumphant Markets*. Belief in solidarity is a characteristic value of the *Hundred Flowers, Shared Responsibilities* and *Creative Societies*, but in fundamentally different ways. Solidarity is predominantly, or exclusively, of a local nature in the *Hundred Flowers*, where large organizations, including the nation state, are increasingly unable to act. In *Shared Responsibilities*, by contrast, solidarity is one of the values at the basis of the regeneration of the public sector. In *Creative Societies*, the values of solidarity are among the motivations of the revolt against the prevailing economic rationality. While all these scenarios can be seen as a continuation of trends already under way, *Turbulent Neighbourhoods* represents a sort of regression, as the preoccupation with security and the need for protection against violence become paramount in a climate of armed conflict.

POLITICS

The increasing importance of the regional level relative to the national level is a trend running across most scenarios. The devolution of powers takes place in orderly fashion in the *Shared Responsibilities* scenario, whereas in the *Hundred Flowers* it is the result of a generalized crisis of large organizations. Another trend common to several scenarios is the clash between 'new' politicians, be it of the free market kind or of more social leanings, and the traditional bureaucracies, with the former emerging on top. In *Triumphant Markets*, the solution involves a drastic downsizing of the state. The *Creative Societies* scenario is one of revolution, implying a total renewal of the political elites. Finally, *Turbulent Neighbourhoods* is a scenario of regression also in the political domain, as the state reasserts itself as the guarantor of external security and the enforcer of law.

ADMINISTRATION

The reform of public administration is at the centre of *Shared Responsibilities*, in which the traditional hierarchical apparatus of government gives way to more horizontal structures, relying increasingly on evaluation and dialogue with the different social actors rather than on command. In this respect, however, there are similarities with the outcome of *Creative Societies*, where the democratic-egalitarian imperative and the clash between administrative cultures are much stronger. In *Triumphant Markets*, administrative reform is driven almost exclusively by the pressure to reduce costs and to make room for the private sector. Finally, little reform occurs in the *Hundred Flowers* and in *Turbulent Neighbourhoods*: in the former, the lack of reform results in national bureaucracies becoming increasingly irrelevant; in the latter, national bureaucracies successfully resist reform in the wake of the security concerns engendered by the war.

GENERAL PUBLIC

Increasing public participation in social and political life is a key element of both *Shared Responsibilities* and *Creative Societies*. The relationship between state and society, however, is always co-operative in the former, initially adversarial in the latter. Public passivity towards politics characterizes the three other scenarios to different degrees. In *Triumphant Markets*, it is linked to the privatization of public functions, while in the *Hundred Flowers* it is the counterpart of the withdrawal into local life. In *Turbulent Neighbourhoods*, by contrast, political passivity co-exists with a broad-based support for the state, consistent with regression toward a more authoritarian model of governance.

EU INSTITUTIONS

In virtually all the scenarios (the only exception being the *Hundred Flowers*), an initial limited reform of the institutions occurs at the beginning of the century, more or less in line with existing engagements. After this, however, institutional patterns diverge. In *Triumphant Markets*, the EU becomes increasingly identified with the Single Market at the expense of the broader political dimension (the term 'EEAization' refers to the European Economic Area, which is the existing institutional arrangement by which the rules of the Single Market are extended to non-EU member countries like Norway and Iceland). This removes some of the obstacles to the enlargement process, which by the year 2010 is supposed to encompass all the existing candidates (the ten Central and Eastern European countries, Cyprus, Malta and Turkey) as well as the remaining countries in the European Free Trade Area (EFTA) and possibly some South-Eastern European countries. In the *Hundred Flowers*, by contrast, the crisis of the Member States translates into paralysis at EU level, with no institutional reform and increasingly acrimonious disputes over the budget. As a result, the enlargement to Central and Eastern Europe is blocked half way. The most ambitious reform of the EU institutions occurs in the *Shared Responsibilities* scenario, consistent with the reform movement at the level of the Member States and the needs of an enlarged EU. The political dimension of the EU is reinforced not only in the realm of foreign and security policy, where the EU becomes increasingly able to speak with one voice, but also through a broad institutional reform. This involves, for example, assigning each country in the Council to one of the three groups (*collegia*) of large, medium-sized and small countries, with the majority of the *collegia* being required for a measure to be passed. Above all, the reform translates into increased decentralization and transparency of EU operations, with the strengthening of local EU offices and the opening of the preparatory and implementation phase of decisions to the instances of civil society. In *Creative Societies*, most of the reform occurs at the level of the Member States, notably in the area of social regulation and taxation, with the EU seconding the movement toward a 'red-green' Europe. Enlargement takes the back seat, at least temporarily, as the EU is absorbed in its own domestic revolution. Finally, in the *Turbulent Neighbourhoods* scenario, the evolution of EU institutions is shaped by the armed conflict in the neighbourhood (the 'Thirst War') and the military involvement of the EU, with the bigger Member States asserting their dominance. On the enlargement front, the cleavage between the 'ins' and the 'outs' becomes deeper and virtually unbridgeable.

LABOUR MARKET AND SOCIAL POLICIES

Triumphant Markets, Shared Responsibilities and *Creative Societies* are scenarios of radical reform in the field of labour market and social policies. In *Triumphant Markets*, following the failure of the social-democratic experiments of the turn of the century, US-style deregulation prevails, with increasing individualization of industrial relations and radical downsizing of the safety nets. In *Shared Responsibilities*, the European corporatist model stages a successful comeback, including a managed deregulation of labour markets accompanied by welfare-to-work reform of social protection. *Creative Societies* provides the most radical alternative to the existing social institutions, as the social economy takes centre stage and social protection is reformed to encourage participation. The reforms also include a radical overhaul of accounting systems, both economy-wide and at the level of the firm, and an accompanying re-organization of taxation. The *Hundred Flowers* and *Turbulent Neighbourhoods*, by contrast, are characterized by relative inertia on labour markets and social policies, at least on a European scale. This is consistent with the increasing differentiation of national and regional situations in the *Hundred Flowers*, with the national level losing control in some countries, and with the absorption with security preoccupations in *Turbulent Neighbourhoods*.

OTHER ECONOMIC POLICIES

The EMU framework remains in place, but the accompanying conditions differ sharply across scenarios. EMU works smoothly in the *Triumphant Markets* and *Shared Responsibilities* scenarios. In the former, there are no glitches because the shrinking of public budgets and the individualization of industrial relations relieve two of the main sources of pressure on monetary policy, namely fiscal pressure and wage pressure. In the latter, EMU works smoothly because of the development of effective economic co-ordination to enhance growth and stability, including an EU cyclical stabilization mechanism to guard against the risk of asymmetric shocks. Less propitious conditions for EMU prevail in the other scenarios, notably during the political uprisings that accompany *Creative Societies*. *Creative Societies* and (for different reasons) *Turbulent Neighbourhoods* are also scenarios in which the independence of the European Central Bank is put increasingly into question by politicians wishing to re-assert their role as representatives of the people's will. In terms of other economic policies, *Shared Responsibilities* is based on a successful role for the public sector as a vehicle for the apprenticeship of new technologies, notably through the provision of content for the new media. *Creative Societies* is also a scenario of radical policy reform, particularly in the areas of taxation and social protection, with the aim of penalizing pollution and promoting the social economy. By contrast, little policy reform occurs in the *Hundred Flowers* and *Turbulent Neighbourhoods*: in the former because of the general crisis of central governments, in the latter because economic policies are conditioned by security concerns. In both cases the functioning of the Single Market is seriously affected.

GLOBALIZATION

In economic terms at least, *Triumphant Markets* is the most favourable to the rapid advance of globalization as all the major areas of the world increasingly share the same politico-economic outlook, largely shaped by the United States. In *Shared Responsibilities*, progress on trade and investment liberalization is matched by the increasing influence of regional groupings in shaping the international economic order. The increasing assertiveness of the EU in this scenario leads to frequent clashes with the United States. Globalization loses some of its momentum in the other three scenarios. In the *Hundred Flowers*, globalization continues to advance where technology is the main driving factor (for example, internet transactions) but is hampered elsewhere by the lack of political will to reach and enforce new agreements. In *Creative Societies* and *Turbulent Neighbourhoods*, by contrast, there is an explicit political will to slow down globalization, linked to societal concerns in the former, to old-fashioned protectionism in the latter. With the exception of *Turbulent Neighbourhoods*, all the scenarios envisage an increasing international role for non-governmental organizations and the emerging global civil society.

REGIONAL SECURITY

Continent-wide market liberalization in *Triumphant Markets* opens up prospects for a good economic performance for the most dynamic regions. Lack of positive political action results in a failure to deal with mounting security threats in and around the enlarged Union. Failure to act in time to stem the tide of rising instability and tension is also a dominant feature in *Turbulent Neighbourhoods*, where the EU subsequently has to resort to muscular military action to restore peace. Fragmentation and erosion of the nation-state of the *Hundred Flowers* are accompanied by a spreading influence of criminal networks and rising ethnic tension in parts of Europe, which leads to occasional outbreaks of violence, often of a local nature. Inward-looking, absorbed by revolutionary zeal, the EU fails to mount stable political co-operation frameworks in *Creative Societies*. After the EU returns to normality again, measures are taken to improve regional stability throughout Europe. In *Shared Responsibilities*, the EU attaches great importance to the fact that enlargement to Central and Eastern Europe and Cyprus is accompanied by the building of solid 'partnerships' with the countries/regions in the enlarged Union's neighbourhood. Regional security is enhanced slowly but surely by an improved socio-economic situation and efforts to strengthen democracy.

CENTRAL AND EASTERN EUROPE

In terms of economic development, Central and Eastern Europe is part of the economic dynamics of *Triumphant Markets*. The development is uneven as some countries, regions or big cities emerge among the most dynamic in Europe while others are marked by backwardness and weak foreign direct investment. The socio-economic development is also uneven in the *Hundred Flowers* where some parts of Central and Eastern Europe suffer from rising inequalities and infiltration from organized criminal networks or unscrupulous politicians. Regional identities are becoming more pronounced, bordering on aggressive ethnicity in some cases. *Turbulent Neighbourhoods* marks a sharp distinction between the most advanced countries in Central and Eastern

Europe which manage to adhere to the EU before the outbreak of war in Europe's neighbourhood, while other countries are trapped in a spiral of acute instability and negative socio-economic development. *Shared Responsibilities* is the scenario that offers the brightest socio-economic and democratic prospects for the countries of Central and Eastern Europe firmly established as members of the EU and with a continued favourable socio-economic development across the board. The red/green reform in *Creative Societies* leads to profound misunderstandings on the direction of society, in particular in social and environmental areas, between Western and Eastern Europe.

MEDITERRANEAN

Regional stability and economic performance broadly go hand in hand also in the Mediterranean, with *Triumphant Markets* and *Shared Responsibilities* offering the best prospects for an improved socio-economic situation in the area. The exclusive focus on trade and investment relations in the *Triumphant Markets* scenario, however, leaves largely untouched important problems such as the environment. In the other scenarios, mediocre or bad economic performance coupled with lack of political attention in Europe contribute to a worsening situation in the Mediterranean, including a deterioration in economic development, a worsening social situation as well as a vicious circle of Islamic terrorism and military repression.

UNITED STATES

The US is set to remain the dominant superpower in the timeframe of the exercise, but its economic and political behaviour differs significantly across scenarios. *Triumphant Markets* is clearly the scenario in which the perspective of the world is modelled on the US, notably through its superior economic performance, and with little requirement for overt military action. In the other scenarios, even if US economic performance ranges from satisfactory (*Shared Responsibilities*) to mediocre (*Turbulent Neighbourhoods*), there is a common trend towards a disengagement of the US from political and military commitments in the rest of the world and especially in Europe. This trend is linked to the emergence of elites that are less focused, because of their origins and culture, on the transatlantic partnership. Only in *Turbulent Neighbourhoods*, however, does political detachment, coupled with economic difficulties, turn into overt isolationism.

RUSSIA

The economic fate of Russia appears linked to that of the industrial world, at least in the sense that, without a satisfactory economic performance world-wide, opportunities for economic recovery in Russia are non-existent. This means that *Triumphant Markets* and *Shared Responsibilities* are the scenarios in which Russia fares relatively better, too. Economic recovery in these two scenarios is coupled with political stabilization and stronger links with the rest of the world. Relations with the EU have clearly a relatively greater role in the *Shared Responsibilities* scenario, where a distinctive European foreign and security policy takes shape gradually. The other scenarios are less positive for Russia and its relations with the rest of the world, ranging from domestic muddling through and estrangement towards Europe in the *Hundred Flowers* and *Creative Societies*, to increasing political and economic disintegration in *Turbulent Neighbourhoods*.

ASIA

Consistent with developments in the rest of the world, *Triumphant Markets* and *Shared Responsibilities* are the scenarios where Asia is best able to maintain a high-growth path. In the former, this means embracing the 'Anglo-Saxon' model of capitalism in the framework of US-led economic liberalization, whereas in the latter there is a tendency toward economic and political re-centring around regions, which allows for a more distinctively Asian identity also in economic organization. The economic transition toward an industrial (and post-industrial) economy is more difficult in the other scenarios, especially in *Turbulent Neighbourhoods*, where worldwide recession and protectionism hit Asia particularly badly. In *Creative Societies*, the most advanced Asian countries show interest in Europe's 'post-modern experiment' (e.g. Japan, South Korea and possibly some Chinese provinces). China is the pivotal force in the region, but in more or less all the scenarios it has to cope with centrifugal tendencies, equally engendered by growth or the lack of it. The relative decline of Japan reflects deep structural trends, including demography, as well as persistent inability to forge strong political links in the region.

8. How we built the scenarios (methodology)

The building of the *Scenarios Europe 2010* followed a methodology called *Shaping Actors-Shaping Factors*. Its development has benefited from regular contacts between the Forward Studies Unit and numerous international institutes active in future studies. In particular, we would like to mention the French Conservatoire National des Arts et Métiers (NAM), the Dutch institute Clingendael, the Anglo-American Global Business Network, the German think-tank EUCIS, the association Futuribles International and strategic think-tanks of large companies such as Shell. The Unit also maintains close contacts with planning and future studies departments in EU Member States and large international organizations, such as the OECD.

The basic sequencing of the construction of the *Scenarios Europe 2010* is similar to the methods developed and used by Futuribles and CNAM and sometimes referred to as the école française (analysis of variables, partial scenarios, global scenarios). The brainstorming methods that were used are closer to the Anglo-Saxon tradition. Furthermore, the objective of the exercise and the fact that it was organized within an institution like the European Commission led the Unit to break new ground with regard to the existing methods. This included the writing up in full of the *partial scenarios* as well as the technique used for the final selection of the *global scenarios*.

The production of the partial scenarios worked as follows. Five themes were chosen for their capacity to capture and illustrate developments relevant for the future of Europe and its process of integration. They were: institutions and governance; social cohesion; economic adaptability; enlargement of the EU; and Europe's external environment. For each theme a working group was created, comprising 12 to 15 Commission officials chosen for their competence on the subject and their interest in a scenario exercise. Each working group was co-ordinated by a member of the Forward Studies Unit and the co-ordinator of the project was involved with the five groups to ensure consistency. A total of over 60 officials took part in the exercise (see Chapter 11). The process was designed so as to encourage participants to 'think aloud' and for group dynamics to generate contrasting mental pictures about the future. At the same time, to ensure control of the process and consistency of output, the methodology followed by each working group was broadly the same. Specifically, the production of the partial scenarios can be described as a six-step process:

1. Kick-off paper: to start the discussion, the co-ordinators present a paper illustrating the main facts about the theme under consideration and putting relevant questions about the future.

2. Selection of variables: the group holds a brainstorming exercise to put together a fairly comprehensive list of the variables that can have an impact on the theme under consideration. Each variable is subsequently classified as factor or actor. Factors are defined as the structural trends that are considered important in shaping future outcomes (in considering each trend, one should bear in mind also the possibility of shocks and inflection points). Actors are defined as those players that can influence factors in an interactive fashion. They are recognizable, purpose-oriented variables, as opposed to the structural and diffuse character of factors. Through reflection and discussion, the initial list of variables (typically numbering around 50) is reduced to a more manageable set (10 to 15).

3. Construction of 'mini-scenarios'. A questionnaire is submitted to each member of the working group, in which they are asked to sketch alternative paths of evolution for each shaping actor or factor. The answers are elaborated to yield comparable sets of alternatives. In practice, this means producing alternative 'stories' (each summarized in a two-line sentence) for each actor/factor. These receive the name of 'mini-scenarios'. Figure 8.1 shows the actors/factors selected for the theme of economic adaptability and the titles of the 'mini-scenarios' corresponding to each actor/factor.

4. Selection of the 'pivot variables'. The actors/factors considered with their alternatives are still too numerous to allow the formation of contrasted pictures of the future. Each group is asked to concentrate on a smaller number of variables which are most liable to make the difference between the possible versions of the future. To facilitate the choice, each factor/actor can be ranked along two dimensions: uncertainty and impact. Those variables that score the highest on both dimensions are selected as 'pivot variables'. This allows concentrating on five to six variables instead of 10–15.

5. Selection of the scenarios. Taking into account only the pivot variables, the group selects a number (typically ranging from six to eight) of plausible and consistent combinations of the 'mini-scenarios'. This means that each combination contains one mini-scenario (in some cases a mix of two mini-scenarios) for each 'pivot variable' and that the mini-scenarios are considered to fit well with each other across the variable spectrum. An

1. Demography	2. Technology/Organization	3. Culture/Values	4. Globalization	5. Macroeconomic policies (EMU)	6. Industrial policies	7. Social and employment policies	8. International regulations	9. European integration	10. Public actors	11. Trade unions	12. NGOs	13. Transnational corporations
Low population growth, medium participation growth	No major breakthrough. Downsizing. Continuing despecialization of Europe in high-tech	Increasing individualism. Fear of the future	Globalization continuing, sectoral resistances, local difficulties	Broad EMU with limited co-ordination and no major tensions	'Horizontal' policies (competitiveness approach)	Continuing 'decremental' adjustment of social protection	Mixed strength of institutions	Broad enlargement, deep integration	Governments constrained by interdependence and lack of consensus	Continuing decline. Persistence in protected sectors	Not significant economic role	TNCs increasingly important
Low population growth, high participation growth, openness to emigration	No major breakthrough. Increasing dualism. Increasing de-specialization of Europe in high-tech	Strongly increasing individualism. Social and geographical segregation. Power of lobbies	Globalization accelerating. 'Borderless world'	Broad EMU with limited co-ordination and major tensions	Acceleration of deregulation and privatization	Strong labour market deregulation. Residual welfare state	Mixed strength of institutions. Increasing regionalism	Broad enlargement, shallow integration	Downsizing of government	Terminal decline	Significant economic role	Declining corporative advantage of TNCs (multinational SMEs)
Low population growth, low participation growth, closure to emigration	Major breakthrough. Europe innovating and/or catching up	Renaissance of social/ecological awareness. Regions/localities experiments	Globalization slowing down, trade conflicts, regional blocks	Broad EMU with strong co-ordination	'New' industrial policies (focus on users)	Strong resistance against welfare state reform	Weak institutions. Reversal of liberalization	Narrow enlargement, deep integration	Institutional renewal	Decline reversal (new corporatism)	Very significant economic role (taking over welfare state)	Political reaction against TNCs
	Major breakthrough. Increasing technologically-induced inequality. Europe catching up	Revolt of the bottom-half against globalization	Global crisis	Failure of EMU	'Mercantilistic' industrial policies	Radical reform of welfare state: universalism and individual incentives	Strong global institutions (economic security council)	Failure of enlargement	Paralysis			
	Major breakthrough. Increasing technologically-induced inequality. Europe falling behind											

Figure 8.1 Working group on economic adaptability actors/factors and mini-scenarios

appropriate title is chosen for each combination. Figure 8.2 presents two examples drawn from the working group on economic adaptability: the white boxes indicate the mini-scenarios which are retained for each of the pivot variables (note that only five variables are considered instead of the 13 in the previous figure). Once the working group is satisfied with the selection of combinations, the other (non-pivot) variables are attached to each combination, as it subjectively seems fit. Finally, through a process of merging and elimination, the combinations selected are reduced to five. Each of these five combinations of mini-scenarios provides the 'skeleton' for a different scenario.

6. Writing of the partial scenarios. Based on the 'skeleton' of mini-scenarios, a script (about 3,000 words long) is produced to give narrative form to each scenario.

Each working group having produced a set of five partial scenarios (five scenarios on governance, five scenarios on social cohesion, etc.), the Forward Studies Unit moved to the second stage of the *Scenarios* project, namely the production of global scenarios. This stage was co-ordinated and implemented by the three authors of the present publication. They were assisted by a steering group including ten other colleagues from the Forward Studies Unit and other departments in the European Commission, all of which had been already involved in the first stage. The production of the global scenarios involved the following six steps:

1. Consistency ranking of the combinations of partial scenarios: in principle, each global scenario can be seen as a combination of five partial scenarios, one for each theme. The theoretical number of such combinations, however, is extremely high. An apposite technique is used to rank the possible combinations for overall consistency, so that only those combinations exhibiting a sufficiently high degree of consistency are retained for further consideration.[1]

2. Selection of the global scenarios. Concentrating on the combinations retained from the consistency exercise, the steering group retains the eight to ten more salient and consistent combinations. This means not only that the partial scenarios contained in each combination should not appear to contradict each other, but also that there should be some salient feature that clearly distinguishes each combination from the others. The combinations are reduced to five through a process of merging and elimination. These five combinations provide the 'skeletons' for the global scenarios.

3. Analysis of the key drivers of the global scenarios: based on a re-reading of the partial scenarios, a number of key drivers, recurring in the different

Partial Scenario 2: Laissez-faire

2. Technology/Organization	3. Culture/Values	4. Globalization	5. Macro-economic policies (EMU)	7. Social and employment policies
No major breakthrough. Downsizing. Continuing despecialization of Europe in high-tech.	Increasing individualism. Fear of the future.	Globalization continuing, sectoral resistances, local difficulties.	Broad EMU with limited co-ordination and no major tensions.	Continuing 'decremental' adjustment of social protection.
No major breakthrough. Increasing dualism of organization. Increasing despecialization of Europe in high-tech.	Strongly increasing individualism. Social and geographical segregation. Power of lobbies.	Globalization accelerating 'Borderless world'.	Broad EMU with limited co-ordination and major tensions.	Strong labour market deregulation. Residual welfare state.
Major breakthrough. Europe innovating and/or catching up.	Renaissance of social/ecological awareness. Regions, localities experiments.	Globalization slowing down, trade conflicts, regional blocks.	Broad EMU with strong co-ordination.	Strong resistance against welfare-state reform.
Major breakthrough. Increasing technologically, induced inequality. Europe catching up.	Revolt of the bottom-half against globalization.	Global crisis.	Failure of EMU.	Radical reform of welfare state, universalism and individual incentives.
Major breakthrough. Increasing technologically, induced inequality. Europe falling behind.				

Partial Scenario 5 (a): Europe's renaissance

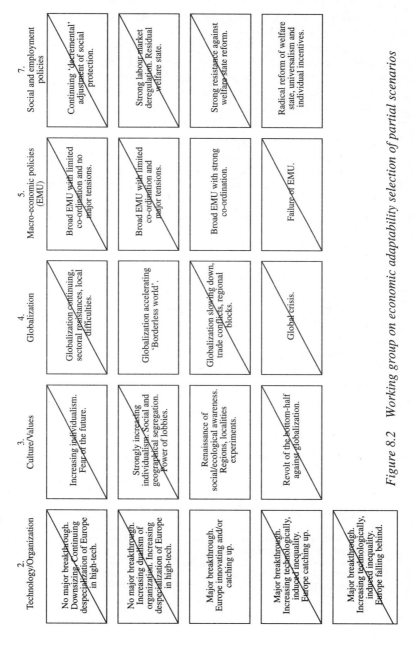

2. Technology/Organization	3. Culture/Values	4. Globalization	5. Macro-economic policies (EMU)	7. Social and employment policies
No major breakthrough. Downsizing. Continuing despecialization of Europe in high-tech.	Increasing individualism. Fear of the future.	Globalization continuing, sectoral resistances, local difficulties.	Broad EMU with limited co-ordination and no major tensions.	Continuing 'decremental' adjustment of social protection.
No major breakthrough. Increasing dualism of organization. Increasing despecialization of Europe in high-tech.	Strongly increasing individualism. Social and geographical segregation. Power of lobbies.	Globalization accelerating 'Borderless world'.	Broad EMU with limited co-ordination and major tensions.	Strong labour-market deregulation. Residual welfare state.
Major breakthrough. Europe innovating and/or catching up.	Renaissance of social/ecological awareness. Regions, localities experiments.	Globalization slowing down, trade conflicts, regional blocks.	Broad EMU with strong co-ordination.	Strong resistance against welfare-state reform.
Major breakthrough. Increasing technologically, induced inequality. Europe catching up.	Revolt of the bottom-half against globalization.	Global crisis.	Failure of EMU.	Radical reform of welfare state, universalism and individual incentives.
Major breakthrough. Increasing technologically, induced inequality. Europe falling behind.				

Figure 8.2 Working group on economic adaptability selection of partial scenarios

working groups, are selected. The role of the key drivers is succinctly described for each global scenario. Contradictions and lacunas are identified and eliminated.

4. Test presentation of 'skeleton' scenarios. Based on the 'skeleton' for the global scenarios, a visual presentation is prepared for the purpose of discussion with test groups, both inside and outside the institution. (Ten presentations were organized within the Commission and twenty were given to outside audiences from Europe, the US and Asia.) Criticisms and comments are collected, examined and, if deemed appropriate, incorporated in the scenarios.

5. Writing of the global scenarios. Based on the 'skeleton' combinations of partial scenarios and the analysis of key drivers, a script (about 4,000 words long) is prepared to give a narrative form to each global scenario.

6. Finalization of the global scenarios. The draft global scenarios are subjected to two rounds of screening and discussion: first by the authors, then within the steering group. Following that, a final version of the global scenarios is produced for publication.

The two-stage process described above was implemented for the first time in the construction of the *Scenarios Europe 2010*, with innovations being introduced practically at each step. While conceived with the specific subject(s) in mind, the process has proved to be flexible enough to accommodate a wide range of possible topics.[2] The Forward Studies Unit continues to work on applications of the *Shaping Actors-Shaping Factors* method with a view to further improving its scenario-building capabilities.

NOTES

1. The technique works as follows. Let gov, coh, eco, enl, wld stand for the groups of scenarios on governance, social cohesion, the economy, enlargement and the world environment, respectively. The ten possible couples of groups are: gov/coh, gov/eco, gov/enl, gov/wld, coh/eco, coh/enl, coh/wld, eco/enl, eco/wld, enl/wld. As each group contains five scenarios, each couple of groups consists of 25 (5×5) combinations of two individual scenarios, for a total of 250 combinations. Each of these combinations is assigned a score for consistency, ranging from 0 to 5. At this point one can calculate a measure of the overall consistency of each theoretically possible combination of five partial scenarios, by summing up the individual scores of the ten couples of scenarios contained in each combination. An electronic spreadsheet programme makes it easy to perform the calculations and to rank the combinations starting from those with the highest overall score (50).
2. For instance, the Unit's *Shaping Actors Shaping Factors* methodology was used by the Norwegian government for the scenario exercise codenamed *Norway 2030* (started in 1998).

9. Glossary

Terms marked with an asterisk (*) refer to fictitious events/institutions mentioned in a given scenario.

accountability: obligation or willingness to accept the responsibility or to account for one's actions. In the context of public administration, it means rules for public authorities to publicly justify and give access to their activities.

apprenticeship process: process of learning or getting fully acquainted with a new skill or new technique.

area of freedom, security and justice: one of the five objectives mentioned by the **Treaty of Amsterdam** to ensure the free movement of persons in the **European Union** in conjunction with appropriate measures to jointly combat transnational criminal phenomena such as terrorism, drug trafficking and illegal immigration.

artificial intelligence: the capability of a machine to imitate intelligent human behaviour.

ASEAN: see **Association of Southeast Asian Nations**.

Association of Southeast Asian Nations (ASEAN): international (regional) organization established in 1967, currently comprising Indonesia, Laos, Malaysia, Myanmar, the Philippines, Singapore, Thailand, Brunei, Vietnam. It aims to promote trade as well as joint research and technical co-operation among its member states.

Asian values: traditions/concepts of thinking developed in Eastern philosophy and specific to Asian societies, such as: moderating the individual's aspirations against the whole of society (human responsibilities as opposed to the Western concept of human rights), cyclic (holistic) rather than linear approach towards nature and human development.

Atlantic Alliance: see **North-Atlantic Treaty Organization**.

baby-boom generation: people born during the post-World War II period (up to the first half of the 1960s) which was marked by a particularly high birth-rate in most industrialized societies.

belle époque: culturally flourishing, euphoric years (for the well-off classes) of the beginning of the twentieth century (lasting until the outbreak of World War I).

Berlaymont: headquarters of the **European Commission** in Brussels.

BordEuro*: see Scenario No. 5.

capital mobility: the ability to freely buy and sell financial assets (e.g. deposits, shares, bonds) across borders.

Central and Eastern Europe: in the context of the **EU** accession negotiations the countries of Bulgaria, Czech Republic, Estonia, Hungary, Latvia, Lithuania, Poland, Romania, Slovakia, Slovenia. In geographical terms, it designates a larger area, including both existing **EU** members (e.g. Austria) and non-candidate countries (e.g. Ukraine).

CIS: see **Commonwealth of Independent States**.

civil society: the citizens who are – politically, socially or culturally – playing an active part in society, but who are not necessarily involved in the political and economic decision making.

closer co-operation: mechanism introduced by the **Treaty of Amsterdam** enabling a majority of Member States to deepen co-operation in a certain policy area while leaving the door open for other Member States to join at a later stage. Such enhanced co-operation must not affect the rights or interests of those Member States which do not participate in it.

clientelism: arbitrary behaviour of politicians/civil servants favouring a certain group of persons (their clientele) over the rest of the population.

clocs*: see Scenario No. 4.

Coimbra Group*: see Scenario No. 3.

Cold War: the open yet restricted rivalry which developed after World War II between the United States and the Soviet Union and their respective allies. It ended with the dissolution of the Soviet system of alliances and the Soviet Union in 1989–91.

collective goods: (also called public goods) contrary to standard economic goods, a collective good can serve a small or a large number of persons at the same total cost (non-rivalry) and it is often impossible to exclude anyone from using it once the good has been provided (non-excludability). Typical examples include military defence and environmental protection. Because of their characteristics, collective goods require either governmental intervention or direct supply by the public sector.

Common Agricultural Policy (CAP): one of the main Community policies (accounting for 48 per cent of the Community budget in 1996), aimed at ensuring a common market for **EU** agricultural produce and a level of economic support for the agricultural community. The CAP works through a system of subsidies and quotas for **EU** producers and of levies and other restrictions on imported agricultural produce.

Common Foreign and Security Policy (CFSP): area of **EU** activity introduced by the **Treaty of Maastricht**, including all the means by which the **EU** seeks to exercise influence in foreign affairs (apart from the purely economic or commercial aspects of external relations). It also provides for the eventual framing of a common defence policy.

Commonwealth of Independent States (CIS): association of sovereign states formed in 1991, comprising Russia and 11 (out of the 14) other republics that were formerly part of the Soviet Union (Estonia, Latvia and Lithuania declined to join the CIS). The CIS aims to co-ordinate its members' policies regarding the economy, foreign relations, defence, immigration policies, environmental protection and law enforcement.

consumerism: the emphasis, linked to advertising and marketing efforts, on creating new and increasing consumption needs.

cordon sanitaire strategy: (*cordon sanitaire*: French for 'sanitary border strip') strategy of isolating a problem within a

given geographical area by erecting imper-
meable borders.

Council of Ministers: consisting of the ministers of the Member States (convening in different subject-based configurations), the Council is the **European Union**'s main decision-making body. It has both executive and legislative powers.

credit-rating agencies: agencies specialized in analysing and evaluating the reliability of enterprises/countries in their role as debtors, using certain classification standards (e.g. AAA for top reliability).

currency merger: the linking up of two or more national currencies by (irrevocably) fixing their exchange rates.

customs union: an agreement among two or more nations to eliminate trade restrictions with each other and to adopt a common trade policy (implying, among other things, the adoption of a common external customs tariff).

decentralization: transfer of (public) decision-making from one (central) level to several (regional and/or local) levels.

decentralization of industrial relations: transfer of collective bargaining (on wages, working conditions, etc.) between trade unions and employers from one (national) level to local/firm level.

democratic emancipation: process indicating the popular search for more active and participatory forms of political expression than that provided by voting in general elections or membership of political parties.

demonetization: process indicating the increase of economic activity relying on barter and local currencies, replacing the exchange of goods for a (legally prescribed, common) currency.

deregulation: the policy of opening previously regulated sectors (e.g. utilities, transportation) to competition through liberalization of entry and prices.

diminishing returns: tendency toward decreasing productivity, i.e. output per input employed. It indicates the passing of the optimum input level.

directive:	one of the **European Community**'s legal instruments. It binds the Member States to the results to be achieved, but leaves a margin for manoeuvre as to the form and means of transposing it into the national legal framework.
do-it-yourself (DIY):	productive leisure activity, consisting in the creation (instead of the purchase) or modification of a useful device of whatever kind.
Economic and Monetary Union (EMU):	the process of harmonizing the economic and financial policies of the Member States of the **European Union** in connection with the unification of monetary policies and introduction of a single currency (**euro**).
Economic and Social Committee:	consultative body of the **EU**, currently consisting of 222 members representing employers, trade unionists and 'other fields' of economic and social activity. It has to be heard by the **Council of Ministers** in certain policy fields before a legal act can be passed and may also issue opinions on its own initiative.
employment pacts:	see **local employment pacts**.
EMU:	see **Economic and Monetary Union**.
Estates-General:	(in French *Etats-généraux*) in pre-Revolutionary France, the representative assembly of the three 'estates' or orders of the realm (clergy, nobility and a 'Third Estate' representing the majority of the people). By analogy, an assembly purporting to represent different parts of society.
EU:	see **European Union**.
euro:	see **Economic and Monetary Union**.
Eurocloc*:	see Scenario No. 4.
Euroland:	see **euro zone**.
Euro-Mediterranean partnership:	framework of co-operation between the **EU** and the states of the Southern Mediterranean basin (Algeria, Cyprus, Egypt, Israel, Jordan, Lebanon, Malta, Morocco, Syria, Tunisia, Turkey and 'the Palestine Authority'), which was established by the Barcelona Declaration of November 1995. It includes three main areas (so-called 'baskets'): political dialogue, economic and financial co-operation and cultural co-operation.

European Central Bank (ECB): European institution established by the **Treaty of Maastricht** responsible for the independent conduct of monetary policy in the Member States participating in stage three of **EMU**, at the head and within the framework of the European System of Central Banks (ESCB).

European Commission: the main initiating institution of the **European Union**. In addition to exclusive rights of initiative, the Commission has functions of execution and control of Community policies. It is composed of 20 independent members, who are assisted by an administration made up of Directorates General and specialized departments.

European Community: the public entity which, together with the European Coal and Steel Community (ECSC) and the European Atomic Community (EURATOM), forms the 'European Communities', a body with international legal personality responsible for the so-called 'first pillar' activities of the **European Union**.

European Council: the regular meetings of the Heads of State or Government of the **European Union** Member States. It meets at least twice a year. Its objectives are to define general policy guidelines.

European Court of Justice: the main judicial institution of the **European Union** institution with two principal functions: to check whether instruments of the European institutions and of governments are compatible with the Treaties, and, at the request of a national court, to pronounce on the interpretation or the validity of provisions contained in Community law. It is composed of 15 judges assisted by nine advocates-general.

European Parliament (EP): the main representative institution of the **European Union**, the EP is an Assembly composed of 626 members who (since 1979) are elected by direct universal suffrage in all the Member States. It is primarily responsible for exercising democratic scrutiny and control over the Union's decision-making process but it is also associated with the **Council** in the legislative process by means of various procedures. Finally, it shares budgetary powers with the **Council** in voting on the annual budget and overseeing its implementation.

European Security Council*: see Scenario No. 5.

European social model: see **Third way (of Europe)/social market economy**.

European stability pact: see **Pact for Stability and Growth**.

European Union (EU): composed of fifteen Member States (Austria, Belgium, Denmark, Finland, France, Germany, Greece, Ireland, Italy, Luxembourg, the Netherlands, Portugal, Spain, Sweden, the United Kingdom), it works towards and oversees the economic and political integration among these states. Schematically, the European Union can be depicted as a structure supported by three pillars. The first pillar comprises the European Communities and their policies, mainly in the economic and the social domain, including **Economic and Monetary Union** (EMU). The second pillar includes the **common foreign and security policy** (CFSP) and aims to initiate a common defence policy. The third pillar involves **justice and home affairs** (JHA) and attempts to institute common rules concerning external borders, judicial co-operation and the fight against international crime. As opposed to the first, 'communitarian' pillar, the two latter pillars are of an intergovernmental character.

Europol (European Police Office): structure for developing police co-operation between Member States in the prevention and combat of serious forms of international organized crime, such as drug trafficking, money laundering, clandestine immigration networks and terrorism.

Eurosec*: see Scenario No. 5.

Eurovigil*: see Scenario No. 5.

euro zone: area comprising the Member States participating in stage three of EMU.

factor mobility: the ability to move factors of production (capital, labour) freely across borders.

fibre optics: the technology allowing the transmission of vast amount of data, including voice and images, by using the properties of light passing through transparent fibres.

FDI: see **foreign direct investment**.

floating exchange rate: an exchange rate (the price of one nation's currency in terms of another nation's currency) determined through the unrestrictive interaction of supply and demand in the foreign exchange market.

foreign direct investment (FDI): the purchase of financial and physical assets in one country by businesses and residents of another country.

free-trade area (FTA): an agreement among two or more nations to eliminate trade barriers with each other. There is no attempt, however, to adopt a common trade policy with other nations.

G7 (Group of Seven): the seven largest industrial countries in the world: the United States, Britain, France, Italy, Canada, Germany, and Japan – which meet regularly to discuss economic and financial matters. The President of the European Commission takes part in the meetings. The G7 is called G8 when Russia participates (which is now the case for all meetings except finance and nuclear safety).

gated communities: upper-class residential complexes protected against the outside world with gates and other high-security devices.

gazelle: small or medium-sized enterprise characterized by an exceptionally fast rate of expansion. They often operate in **high value added sectors** employing highly qualified staff.

GDP: see **gross domestic product**.

genetic diversity: the existence of a large number of organisms (on earth) having a different biological structure.

globalization: the steady increase in the cross-border flows of trade, investment and financial capital since World War II, and its more recent acceleration as far as the two latter are concerned.

global warming: see **greenhouse effect**.

Golden Age: in the context of economic history, the period after World War II, standing out as an episode of exceptionally fast growth of the industrial economies.

Great Depression: decline in economic activity in North America, Europe and other industrialized countries which began in 1929 and lasted until World War II. It was the longest and most severe economic depression ever experienced by the industrialized world.

green accounting: systematic presentation of data on environmentally important stocks and flows (e.g. stocks of life-sustaining natural resources, flows of pollutants), accompanying conventional economic accounts (e.g measures of **gross domestic product**) with the ultimate objective of providing a comprehensive measure of the environmental consequences of economic activity.

green technologies: technologies designed to minimize the impact of economic activities on the environment, either by being 'clean' or by being efficient.

greenhouse effect: a warming of the Earth's surface and lower atmosphere that tends to intensify with an increase in atmospheric carbon dioxide.

gross domestic product (GDP): the total market value of all goods and services produced within the boundaries of an economy during a given period of time, usually one year.

high value added sector: in general, industries where the value of goods and services sold is high relative to the value of purchased inputs. Typically, they employ highly qualified (and highly remunerated) staff, such as in communications, banking and finance and consulting.

High Representative of the EU for the Common Foreign and Security Policy: often referred to under the French acronym 'Monsieur PESC'): function established by the **Treaty of Amsterdam** to assist the Presidency of the **Council of Ministers** in formulating, preparing and implementing decisions relating to the **EU**'s **Common Foreign and Security Policy (CFSP)**. The High Representative is also Secretary General of the **Council**.

hinterland:	region falling within the sphere of influence of a (politically and/or economically) more powerful region.
human capital:	the sum total of a person's productive knowledge, experience and training.
ICT:	see **information and communication technologies**.
IGC:	see **intergovernmental conference**.
Industrial Revolution:	in modern history, the change from an agrarian, handicraft economy to one dominated by industry and machine manufacture.
informal economy (underground economy):	the total of economic activities that – while lawful in nature – are not declared to the public authorities, typically to avoid taxes and regulatory constraints. Prudential estimates of the size of the informal economy in the EU vary between 7 per cent and 16 per cent of **GDP**.
information and communication technologies (ICTs):	technologies allowing the electronic processing and transmission of information.
information technologies (ITs):	technologies aimed at the electronic processing of information, comprising computer hardware and software, databases and related know-how.
intangible goods:	products in the form of codified information and (scientific, literary, artistic) creations, which can be increasingly stocked and traded across distance by using **information and communication technologies**.
intergovernmental approach (intergovernmentalism):	institutional arrangements and decision-making procedures on the **EU** level that are marked by the Member States' dominance in initiating, deciding and executing European policies. Characteristics are **unanimity voting** in the **Council of Ministers** and a minimum of involvement of the other (supranational) Community institutions (**European Commission, European Parliament**) in the decision-making process.
intergovernmental conference (IGC):	the formal negotiations between the Member States' governments with a view to amending the Treaties.
intergovernmentalism:	see **intergovernmental approach**.

isolationism: a traditional strain in the United States' politics pleading for the non-involvement of US foreign policy and defence in matters outside the American hemisphere.

IT: see **information technology**.

JHA: see **justice and home affairs**.

justice and home affairs (JHA): EU co-operation in the fields of asylum policy, immigration policy, combating drugs, combating international fraud, judicial and police co-operation. Its objective is the establishment of an **area of freedom, security and justice**.

knowledge society: society in which knowledge is the most important attribute of economic and social activities, implying the need for individuals to constantly maintain and improve their **human capital**.

least developed countries: (also low-income economies) countries whose level of **per capita** gross national product (GNP) falls below a low threshold. According to the classification adopted by the World Bank, low-income economies are those having a **per capita** GNP of $725 or less.

legitimacy: the installation and/or justifiability of a political system according to certain, above-all democratic, standards. Legitimacy is closely linked to the concept of **accountability**.

Lifelong learning: the idea and practice of learning as a permanent activity throughout the life span of an individual.

Local employment pacts: negotiating mechanisms to bring together the main actors in a regional economy (enterprises, trade unions, local and regional authorities, etc.) with the objective of increasing employment.

macro-economic indicators: measures of economic aggregates such as **GDP**, inflation and unemployment, which taken together give a picture of the 'state of health' of the economy.

majority voting: refers to the decision-making procedure in the **Council of Ministers**. Majority voting may be simple majority or **qualified majority voting** (the most frequent case).

marginal product: in a production process, the increase in output obtained by adding one unit of a productive

	factor, while keeping the quantity of other factors unchanged.
Member of Parliament (MP):	member of a national Parliament.
Member of the European Parliament (MEP):	one of the 626 members of the **European Parliament**.
MEP:	see **Member of the European Parliament**.
multilateral institution:	international organization, the membership of which is potentially open to all states, aiming to foster co-operation in specific areas.
multiple belongings:	sociological notion describing the fact that an individual feels equally close or loyal towards several, for example geographic, entities.
NAFTA:	see **North-American Free-Trade Agreement**.
NATO:	see **North-Atlantic Treaty Organization**.
neo-liberalism:	political current advocating the deregulation of the markets and a withdrawal of the state from the economy.
new information technologies (NITs):	see **information technologies**.
NGO:	see **non-governmental organization**.
non-cash economy:	economic activities – often in the **informal economy** – that do not rely on money as a means of exchange.
non-governmental organization (NGO):	private-sector, mostly non-profit organization active in specific issue area (e.g. development, human rights, environment, fight against social exclusion). NGOs often act as pressure groups.
non-market activity:	production of goods and services that is not carried out for sale on the market. It includes services provided by the state or the non-profit sector on a universal or need basis as well as production for self-consumption.
non-military security:	see **soft security**.
non-profit sector:	(also called third sector) non-public, independent organizations, active in various areas but notably in health, social and education services, and characterized by the absence of the profit objective and the reliance on a certain level of voluntary work/contribution.
non-traded sector:	part of the economy producing goods and services that are not traded internationally.

North-American Free-Trade Agreement (NAFTA):	trade pact signed in 1992 providing the gradual elimination of most tariffs and other trade barriers between the United States, Canada and Mexico, effectively creating a free-trade area.
North-Atlantic Treaty Organization (NATO):	collective defence organization originally established in 1949 as a counterweight to the Soviet military presence in Eastern Europe. It currently includes 19 members: Belgium, Canada, the Czech Republic, Denmark, France, Germany, Greece, Hungary, Iceland, Italy, Luxembourg, the Netherlands, Norway, Poland, Portugal, Spain, Turkey, the United Kingdom, the United States of America.
OAU:	see **Organisation of African Unity**.
OCOMED* (Organisation for Mediterranean Co-operation):	see Scenario No. 3.
one-stop shop approach:	administrative practice by which a user can go through formalities necessary for obtaining a public service (for example unemployment benefit) at a single service point.
opt-out:	the possibility for a contracting party to choose not to commit itself by a certain provision of a treaty.
orderly default:	the unilateral repudiation by the state of implicit financial obligations, e.g. by successively revising downward pension benefits payable to currently working generations.
Organization of African Unity (OAU):	established in 1963, it comprises 53 of the 54 countries of Africa (Morocco withdrew in 1985). Its primary aim is to promote unity and solidarity among African countries, including improving the general living standards, defending the territorial integrity and independence of African states, and promoting international co-operation.
outsourcing:	the decision to rely on external suppliers for activities that were previously carried out within the company. In some cases outsourcing involves moving activities with relatively low value added towards low-wage countries.

Pact for Stability and Growth (Stability and Growth Pact): agreement – formalized in a **European Community** regulation – setting out the rules for budgetary behaviour in stage three of **Economic and Monetary Union (EMU)**. In particular, it specifies how the countries participating in **EMU** should conform to the 3 per cent limit on budget deficits set in the **Treaty of Maastricht** and the sanctions attached to the non-respect of that limit.

PAFTA*: see **Pan-American Free-Trade Agreement**.

Pan-American Free-Trade Agreement (PAFTA)*: see Scenario No. 5.

paradigm shift: change of the fundamental framework of scientific approach to a phenomenon, for example in sociology the shift from the 'modern' to the 'post-modernist' paradigm.

per capita: 'per head', that is, divided by the number of the population of a given country, e.g. **GDP** per capita.

Planet Round*: see Scenario No. 1.

post-modernism: refers to a **paradigm shift** in the sociological characterization of Western societies since the second half of the twentieth century. Its main elements include a decline in tradition values (e.g. respect for established authorities) and a rise in universal **individualism**.

prime-age: workers typically between 30 and 55 years of age, who tend to be favoured in terms of salary and other entitlements compared to younger and older workers.

qualified majority voting (QMV): voting rule in the **Council of Ministers** entailing giving each Member State a weighted number of votes ranging from two for the smallest state to ten for the largest.

Quirinale: official residence of the Italian President in Rome.

R & D: see **research & development**.

regional bloc: a group of countries belonging to the same geographical region and co-operating more or less closely on economic or political matters. The expression 'regional bloc' can have an antagonistic connotation (e.g. during the **Cold War** the Soviet bloc vs. the Western bloc).

representative democracy: a form of democracy based primarily on representation, i.e. the election by the people of parliamentarians who will conduct and monitor political business in their name. It is to be compared with 'participative democracy', where the people are expected to play a more direct role in policy making in addition to their right to vote (e.g. through their involvement in **civil society**).

research & development (R&D): systematic study directed towards fuller scientific knowledge and systematic use of this knowledge for the production of useful materials, devices, systems or methods.

rule of law: a legal and political system in which all actions of the state can only be taken according to prefixed constitutional or statutory rules and where effective legal remedies are provided for in case of non-compliance of a representative of the state with these prefixed rules.

Schengen: agreements between EU Member States aiming at the gradual removal of controls at internal borders and a strengthening of common external borders. The United Kingdom and Ireland are not members of Schengen, while some non-EU countries (Iceland and Norway) are. The **Treaty of Amsterdam** provides for the integration of Schengen into the EU treaties as part of the policy to create an **area of freedom, security and justice**.

secondary education: school education leading up to the admission to university.

service sector: one of the three parts of the economy (together with the agricultural and industrial sectors). Generally speaking, it includes activities that provide direct satisfaction of wants and needs without resulting in physical products or goods (e.g. health, education).

single currency ('euro'): see **Economic and Monetary Union**.

Single Market: the set of rules allowing for the freedom of movement for goods, services, capital and workers within the European Union. The Single

European Act (1986) aimed at facilitating the adoption of rules to implement the Single Market.

Social Europe: the set of policies and actions decided at EU level to promote the individual and collective rights of the workers (employment protection, health and safety ...) and in general to improve the tackling of social problems (e.g. social exclusion).

social market economy: (German *Soziale Marktwirtschaft*) an economy based on market principles in which the state intervenes to protect the weakest members of society, in order to maintain a social balance.

soft security: security threats that are not of a military nature: e.g. international crime, terrorism, environmental risks, arms smuggling, trafficking in drugs or human beings.

Stability (and Growth) Pact: see **Pact for Stability and Growth**.

statutory tax rates: the rate at which a tax is applied on a given income or asset, as prescribed by tax regulations.

structural unemployment: in general terms, that part of unemployment which is not reversed by subsequent economic upturn. It is often identified with the component of unemployment that cannot be influenced by macroeconomic policy (fiscal policy, monetary policy) but requires structural reform of labour markets.

subsidiarity: a guiding principle of federalism stipulating that decisions should be taken at the lowest level consistent with effective action within a political system. Specifically, it is the principle whereby the **European Union** does not take action (except in the areas which fall within its exclusive competence) unless this is more effective than action taken at national, regional or local level.

sustainable development: a model of economic development which takes into account society also in the very long run – particularly the need to control the pressure of human activities on the natural environment and

	to improve the range of people's opportunities, in terms of income, health, education.
tax base:	the part of available income or assets forming the base for the calculation of taxes.
techno crime:	criminality which presupposes advanced skills in **information and communication technologies (ICTs)**, e.g. data pirating, manipulation of computer networks, etc.
tertiary education:	university education.
Third Industrial Revolution:	according to some economists, the appearance of **ICTs** may trigger such a change in the economy and society that it could compare to the First Industrial Revolution (starting towards the end of the eighteenth century, with the introduction of steampower) and the Second Industrial Revolution (starting at the end of the nineteenth century, with the introduction of electric power and the combustion engine).
third way (of Europe):	political idea meaning that Europe should develop its own model between a purely market-oriented economy and a state-managed economy.
total factor productivity:	measure of the efficiency with which capital and labour are employed in the economy or in an industry. It is measured by the weighted average of capital and labour productivity, the weights being the income shares of capital and labour, respectivly.
trade-bloc:	group of geographically close countries which co-ordinate their foreign trade policies.
transparency:	openness and clarity in the daily operation of administrations and institutions, e.g. right to information, public access to official documents, consultation mechanisms, etc.
Treaty of Amsterdam:	in force since May 1, 1999, it constitutes the latest review of the European Union's 'constitutional' framework (see **Treaty of Maastricht**). The main accomplishments of the Treaty are: the introduction of guarantees of specific fundamental rights within the **European Union**; improvements in areas directly concerning the citizens (such as employment, social and

environmental policy); a strengthening of the
EU's instruments in external policy (common
commercial policy and **Common Foreign and
Security Policy**); and some modifications of
the **EU**'s internal procedures (extension of
qualified majority voting, possibility of **closer
co-operation** between member states, enhanced
roles of the **Economic and Social Committee**
and other consultative EU institutions).

Treaty of Gibraltar*: see Scenario No. 5.

Treaty of Maastricht: or Treaty on European Union, entered into force
in November 1993. The Treaty of Maastricht
established the **Economic and Monetary
Union** (**EMU**, ultimately leading to the adoption of the '**euro**') and the **European Union**
(paving the way towards a **Common Foreign
and Security Policy** and co-operation in the
field of **Justice and Home Affairs**).

triumvirate: in Ancient Rome, the periods when power was
exercised by three leaders (first triumvirate =
Pompey, Caesar and Crassus; second triumvirate = Octavius, Antony and Lepidus). By
analogy, a group of three people or countries
exercising power.

UN General Assembly: one of the six principal organs of the **United
Nations (UN)**. The General Assembly, which is
convened yearly or by special session when
necessary, includes representatives of all members of the UN, each nation having one vote.

unanimity voting: the term 'unanimity' refers to the requirement
for all the Member States meeting in the
Council to be in agreement before a proposal
can be adopted. As a consequence, the unanimity procedure gives a Member State the right
to veto a decision. In the policies forming the
first pillar of the **European Union** the application of unanimity voting is restricted and
qualified majority voting applies to most
cases. The second and third pillars, however,
still operate almost exclusively according to the
intergovernmental approach and the unanimity requirement.

underground economy: see **informal economy**.

United Nations (UN): international organization established in 1945 with the purposes of maintaining international peace and security, developing friendly relations among nations and encouraging international co-operation.

universal individualism: sociologists usually make a difference between two aspects of 'individualism': 'particularist individualism', reflecting individuals' will to follow their own desires, regardless of the effect on society; and 'universal individualism', i.e. the principle according to which every person is equal and free to choose his or her way of life as long as the freedom of others and the limits needed for the smooth functioning of the society are respected.

value added: the difference between the value of goods and services sold and that of purchased input. It is equal to the sum of compensation of labour and gross operating surplus.

vocational training: specialized education aiming at the procurement of certain skills or the preparation for a certain activity on the labour market.

wage-price spiral: the mechanism by which wage increases feed into price rises and these in turn, by influencing expectations, prompt further wage increases.

welfare state: concept of government in which the state has a major responsibility in the protection and promotion of the economic and social well-being of its citizens. Specifically, it denominates the set of public policies to protect income against the risks of unemployment, sickness, disability and old age and to provide health care, education and housing.

Westernization: the spreading of Western concepts and values (such as rationalism, the supremacy of the rights of the individual) to non-Western regions of the world.

WEU: Western European Union. Founded in 1948, the WEU is an association of ten Western European nations (who are at the same time **EU** Member States: Belgium, France, Greece, Germany,

Italy, Luxembourg, the Netherlands, Portugal, Spain, and the United Kingdom), plus five observers (Austria, Denmark, Finland, Ireland and Sweden), three associate members (Iceland, Norway and Turkey) and ten associate partners (Bulgaria, Czech Republic, Estonia, Hungary, Latvia, Lithuania, Poland, Romania, Slovakia and Slovenia). It operates as a forum for the co-ordination of matters of European security and defence, in co-operation with **NATO**. It is envisaged to become the **EU**'s defence arm.

working poor: low-wage workers whose income falls below a given poverty threshold.

World Trade Organization (WTO): international organization designed to supervise and liberalize world trade. The WTO, which came into being in 1995 with 104 founding members (currently 136 members), is the successor of the General Agreement of Tariffs and Trade (GATT).

WTO: see **World Trade Organization**.

YES-zone*: see Scenario No. 1.

zero-sum game: a game in which the gains of one player are exactly offset by the losses of the other player(s). By analogy, a situation in which there is no net overall benefit to share.

10. References

Alogoskoufis, G., Bean, C., Bertola, G., Cohen, D., Dolado, J. and Saint-Paul, G. (1995), *Unemployment: Choices for Europe*, CEPR, London.

Amato, G. and Batt, J. (1998), *Minority Rights and EU Enlargement to the East*, Policy Paper No. 98/5, The Robert Schuman Centre, European University Institute, Florence.

Amato, G. and Batt, J. (1999), *The Long-Term Implications of EU Enlargement: Culture and National Identity*, Policy Paper No. 99/1, The Robert Schuman Centre, European University Institute, Florence.

Amato, G. and Batt, J. (1999), *Socio-Economic Discrepancies in the Enlarged EU*, Policy Paper No. 99/2, The Robert Schuman Centre, European University Institute, Florence.

Amato, G. and Batt, J. (1999), *Mobility in an Enlarged European Union*, Policy Paper No. 99/4, The Robert Schuman Centre, European University Institute, Florence.

Andersen Consulting (1998), *Europe Beyond the Millennium. Making Sense of Tomorrow*, Andersen Consulting, London.

Bercusson, B. *et al.* (1996), *A Manifesto for Social Europe*, European Trade Union Institute, Brussels.

Bootle, R. (1997), 'The Death of Inflation', *World Economic Affairs*, Winter.

Bosworth, B. (1996), 'Prospects for Saving and Investment in Industrial Countries', *Future Capital Shortages. Real Threat or Pure Fiction?*, OECD, Paris.

Bosworth, B., Collins, S. and Chen, Y. (1995), 'Accounting for Differences in Economic Growth', *Brookings Discussion Papers in International Economics*, No. 114.

Buti, M., Pench, L.R. and Sestito, P. (1998), *European Unemployment: Contending Theories and Institutional Complexities*, Chief Economist's Department, European Investment Bank, Report 98/01, Luxembourg.

Castel, R. (1995), *Les métamorphoses de la question sociale*, Fayard, Paris.

Central Planning Bureau (1992), *Scanning the Future. A Scenario-Study of the World Economy: 1990–2015*, Central Planning Bureau, The Hague.

Commission on Global Governance (1995), *Our Global Neighbourhood*, Oxford University Press, New York.

Cornia, A. (1998), *Globalisation and Income Distribution*, paper presented at the international seminar 'Globalisation: A Challenge for Peace: Solidarity or Exclusion?' organized by the Instituto Internazionale Jacques Maritain, Milan, 29–31 October.

Cottey, A. (ed.) (1999), *Subregional Co-operation in the New Europe*, The East–West Institute, Macmillan Press, London.

Dehousse, R. (1997), 'Regulation by Networks in the European Community: the Role of Agencies', *Journal of European Public Policy*, No. 4:2, pp. 246–61.

Dehousse, R. (1998), *Citizens' Rights and the Reform of Comitology Procedures: The Case for a Pluralist Approach*, Policy Paper, No. 98/4, The Robert Schuman Centre, European University Institute, Florence.

Delmas, P. (1995), *Le bel avenir de la guerre*, NRF essais, Paris.

Englander, A.S. and Gurney, A. (1994), 'La productivité dans la zone OCDE. Les déterminants à moyen terme', *Revue Économique de l'OCDE*, No. 22.

European Commission (1995), *The Demographic Situation in the European Union*, Luxembourg, OPOCE, Luxembourg.

European Commission (1995) 'Some Implications of Demographic Trends up to 2020', *European Economy*, No. 56.

European Commission (1997), 'Agenda 2000: For a Stronger and Wider Union', *Bulletin of the European Union*, supplement 5/97, OPOCE, Luxembourg.

European Commission (1997), 'Opinions on Hungary's, Poland's, Romania's, Slovakia's, Latvia's, Estonia's, Lithuania's, Bulgaria's, the Czech Republic's and Slovenia's Applications for Membership of the European Union', *Bulletin of the European Union*, supplements 6–15/97, OPOCE, Luxembourg.

European Commission (1997), 'Demographic Report 1997', mimeo.

European Commission (1997), *The Competitiveness of the European Industry*, OPOCE, Luxembourg.

European Commission (1997), 'The Welfare State in Europe. Challenges and Reforms', *European Economy, Reports and Studies*.

European Commission (1998), *Society: The Endless Frontier. A European Vision of Research and Innovation Policies for the 21st Century*, OPOCE, Luxembourg.

European Commission (1998), 'Composite Paper: Progress Made by the Candidate Countries towards Accession', *Bulletin of the European Union*, supplement 4/98, OPOCE, Luxembourg.

European Commission (1998), 'Regular Reports 1998 from the Commission on Hungary's, Poland's, Romania's, Slovakia's, Latvia's, Estonia's, Lithuania's, Bulgaria's, the Czech Republic's, Slovenia's, Cyprus's and Turkey's Progress towards Accession', *Bulletin of the European Union*, supplements 5–16, OPOCE, Luxembourg.

European Commission, Directorate-General 1 and Stiftung Wissenschaft und

Politik (1998), *Illicit Trade and Organised Crime: The Threats to Economic Security*, OPOCE, Luxembourg.

European Commission, Directorate-General 5 (1996), *For a Europe of Civic and Social Rights*, Report by the Comité des Sages, OPOCE, Luxembourg.

European Commission, *Eurobarometer*, various volumes, in particular no. 50 (1999), OPOCE, Luxembourg.

European Commission, Eurostat (1996), *ACP-ALA-MED Basic Statistics*, OPOCE, Luxembourg.

European Commission, Eurostat (1998), *Social Portrait of Europe*, OPOCE, Luxembourg.

European Commission, Forward Studies Unit (Lebessis, N. and Paterson, J.), *Evolutions in Governance: What Lessons for the Commission? A First Assessment*, working paper, forthcoming.

European Commission, Forward Studies Unit (Lebessis, N. and Paterson, J.), *A Learning Society: Proposals for 'Designing Tomorrow's Commission'*, working paper, forthcoming.

European Commission, Forward Studies Unit (Lebessis, N. and Paterson, J.), *The Future of European Regulation: A Review of the Workshop 11 June 1997*, working paper, forthcoming.

European Commission, Forward Studies Unit (Bertrand, G.), *The Union We Need*, working paper, forthcoming.

European Commission, Forward Studies Unit and Fondazione Rosselli, *Organised Criminality and Security in Europe*, working paper, forthcoming.

European Commission, Forward Studies Unit (Michalski, A. and Tallberg, J.), *European Integration Indicators: People's Europe*, working paper, forthcoming.

European Commission, Forward Studies Unit, *Survey on National Identity and Deep-Seated Attitudes to European Integration in Estonia, Latvia, Lithuania, Poland, the Czech Republic, Slovakia, Hungary, Slovenia, Romania, and Bulgaria*, working paper, forthcoming.

European Commission, Forward Studies Unit (1998), *The Future of Russia. Shaping Actors, Shaping Factors*, OPOCE, Luxembourg and Kogan Page, London.

European Commission, Forward Studies Unit (1998), *Towards a More Coherent Global Economic Order*, OPOCE, Luxembourg and Kogan Page, London.

European Commission, Institute for Perspective Technological Studies (1999), 'The Futures Project. Overview', mimeo.

European Parliament (1996), 'Report on Participation of Citizens and Social Players in the Union's Institutional System', PE 218.253/fin., 29 October 1996.

European Union (1997), *Consolidated Treaties*, OPOCE, Luxembourg.

Feenstra, R.C. (1998), 'Integration of Trade and Disintegration of Production in the Global Economy', *Journal of Economic Perspectives*, No. 12.

Finland's Prime Minister's Office (1996), *Finland and the Future of Europe*, Prime Minister's Office, Helsinki.

Freeman, C. and Soete, L (1994), *Work for All or Mass Unemployment?*, Pinter Publisher, London.

Freeman, R.B. (1995), 'Are Your Wages Set in Beijng?', *Journal of Economic Perspectives*, No. 9.

Freeman, R.B. (1996), 'Labor Market Institutions and Earnings Inequality', *New England Economic Review*, May/June (special issue).

Friends of Europe (1999), *A European Union that Works: Blueprint for Reform*, mimeo, Brussels.

Fuhrer, J.C. and Little, J.S. (1996), 'Technology and Growth: an Overview', *New England Economic Review*, Nov./Dec.

Futuribles (1995), 'L'evolution des valeurs des Européens', July/Aug. (special issue), Paris.

Godet, M. (1994), *From Anticipation to Action. A Handbook of Strategic Perspective*, UNESCO, Paris.

Grossman, G.M. (1993), *Pollution and Growth: What Do We Know?*, CEPR, Discussion Paper, No. 848, London.

Herzog, P. (1999), *Manifest pour une démocratie européenne*, Les éditions de l'atelier, Paris.

Holmes, L. (1997), *The Democratic State or State Democracy? Problems of Post-Communist Transition*, Jean Monnet Chair Papers, No. 97/48, The Robert Schuman Centre, European University Institute, Florence.

Inglehart, R. (1995), 'Changing Values, Economic Development and Political Change', *Revue international des sciences sociales* (English edn), No. 145, September, pp. 379–403.

Jacquemin, A. and Pench, L.R. (eds) (1997), *Europe Competing in the Global Economy. Reports of the Competitiveness Advisory Group*, Edward Elgar, Aldershot, UK.

Jacquemin, A. and Wright, D. (eds) (1992), *The European Challenges Post-1992: Shaping Factors, Shaping Actors*, Edward Elgar, Aldershot, UK.

de Jouvenel, H. (1996), 'Changing Europe. An Overview of Broad Economic, Social and Cultural Trends', mimeo.

Karlsson, I. (1996), *Europa och folken: En europeisk nation eller nationernas Europa?*, Wahlström & Widstrand, Stockholm.

Keating, G. and Wilmot, J. (1992), 'The New Regions', *Towards the 21st Century*, No. 2, CS First Boston.

Kennedy, P. (1993), *Preparing for the Twenty-First Century*, HarperCollins, London.

Krugman (1995), 'Growing World Trade: Causes and Consequences', *Brookings Papers on Economic Activity.*

Labohm, H.H.J., Rood, J.Q. Th. and van Staden, A. (1998), *'Europe' on the Threshold of the 21st Century. Five Scenarios*, Netherlands Institute of International Relations, *Clingendael*, The Hague.

Laffan, B. (ed.) (1996), *Constitution-Building in the European Union*, Institute of European Affairs, Dublin.

Laurent, A. (1987), *Histoire de l'individualisme*, PUF, Paris.

Levin, B. and Nordfors, L. (1998), *Vem Tar Makten? Fyra Scenarier med Vinnare och Förlorare i Norden 2008*, Ekerlids Förlag, Stockholm.

Maddison A. (1995), *L'economie Mondiale 1820-1992. Analyse et Statistiques*, OECD, Paris.

Majone, G. (ed.) (1996), *Regulating Europe*, Routledge, London.

Majone, G. (1997), 'The New European Agencies: Regulation by Information', *Journal of European Public Policy*, No. 4:2, pp. 262–75.

Mokyr, J. (1997), 'Are We Living in the Middle of an Industrial Revolution?', *Federal Reserve of Kansas City Economic Review*, No. 82.

Obstfeld, M. (1998), 'The Global Capital market: Benefactor or Menace?', *Journal of Economic Perspectives*, No. 12.

OECD (1994), *Employment/Unemployment Study. Draft Background Report*, OECD, Paris.

OECD (1996), *OECD Economies at a Glance. Structural Indicators*, OECD, Paris.

OECD (1997), 'Towards a New Global Age: Challenges and Opportunities', mimeo, Paris.

Oliner, S.D. and Sichel, D.E. (1994), 'Computers and Output Growth Revisited: How Big Is the Puzzle?', *Brookings Papers on Economic Activity.*

Oman, C. (1994), *Globalisation and Regionalisation. The Challenge for Developing Countries*, The Development Centre, OECD, Paris.

Papademetriou, D. (1996), *Coming Together or Pulling Apart? The European Union's Struggle with Immigration and Asylum*, Carnegie Endowment for International Peace, New York.

Pape, W. (ed.) (1996), *Shaping Factors in East Asia by the Year 2000 and Beyond*, Institute for Asian Affairs, Hamburg.

Pierson, P. (1996), 'The New Politics of the Welfare State', *World Politics*, No. 48.

Politi, A. (1997), *European Security: The New Transnational Risks*, Chaillot Papers, No. 29, Institute for Security Studies, West European Union, Paris.

Porter, M. (1990), *The Competitive Advantage of Nations*, Macmillan, London.

Rhodes, M. (1997), *Globalisation, Labour Markets and Wefare States: A*

Future of Competitive Corporatism?, Working Papers, No. 97/36, The Robert Schuman Centre, European University Institute, Florence.

Richardson, J.D. (1995), 'Income Inequality and Trade: How to Think, What to Conclude', *Journal of Economic Perspectives*, No. 9.

Rochefort, R. (1997), *Les nouveaux modes de vie*, Editions Odile Jacob, Paris.

Scharpf, F. (1997), 'Economic Integration, Democracy and the Welfare State', *Journal of European Public Policy*, No. 4:1, pp. 18–36.

Shepley, S. and Willmot, J. (1992), 'Europe: Core vs Periphery', *Towards the 21st Century*, No. 4, CS First, Boston.

Snower, D.J. (1996), *Challenges to Social Cohesion and Approaches to Policy Reform*, paper prepared for the OECD conference 'Economic Flexibility and Societal Cohesion in the 21st Century', Paris, 16 December 1996.

Snower, D.J. and Lindbeck, A. (1995), 'Restructuring Production and Work', Working Paper, University of London, Birkbeck College, Department of Economics, London.

Soete, L. (Chairman), *High Level Group of Experts* (1997), 'Building the Information Society for Us All', mimeo.

Tanzi, V. and Schuknecht, L. (1995), 'The Growth of Government and the Reform of the State in Industrial Countries', IMF Working Paper.

United Nations (1994), *Human Development Report*, Oxford University Press, Oxford.

Walldén, A.S. (1998), *EU Enlargement: How Much it Will Cost and Who Will Pay*, Occasional Papers, No. 14/98, Hellenic Foundation for European & Foreign Policy (ELIAMEP), Athens.

Weiler, J.H.H. (1997), 'The Reformation of European Constitutionalism', *Journal of Common Market Studies*, Vol. 35, No. 1, pp. 97–131.

Williamson, J.C. (1998), 'Globalisation, Labour Markets and Policy Backlash in the Past', *Journal of Economic Perspectives*, No. 12.

Wood, A. (1995), 'How Trade Hurt Unskilled Workers', *Journal of Economic Perspectives*, No. 9.

World Bank (1996), *Global Economic Prospects and the Developing Countries*, World Bank, Washington DC.

World Bank (1997), *World Development Indicators*, World Bank, Washington DC.

Zinoviev, A. (1995), *L'Occidentisme. Essai sur le triomphe d'une idéologie*, Editions Plon.

11.   Participants in the working groups

The Directorates General or services mentioned are those where people were working at the time of the exercise.

For the purpose of clarity, a list of the Directorates General and their domains of competence follows.

Group 1: Institutions and governance	David Coyne	DG V
	Claire Durand	Legal Service
	Francisco Fonseca Morillo	Treaty of Amsterdam Unit
	Thomas Jansen	Forward Studies Unit
	Patrick Keen	DG III
	Notis Lebessis	Forward Studies Unit
	Michel Magnier	DG IX
	Anna Michalski	Forward Studies Unit
	Agne Pantelouri	Forward Studies Unit
	Vincent Rey	Secretariat General
	Adrian Taylor	DG IB
	Rainer von Leoprechting	DG XIX
	Véronique Warlop	Treaty of Amsterdam Unit
	Jérôme Vignon (co-ord.)	Forward Studies Unit
	Gilles Bertrand	Forward Studies Unit
Group 2: Social and economic cohesion	Vittorio Campanelli	Secretariat General
	Yves Chassard	DG V
	Philippe Doucet	DG XVI
	Constantinos Fotakis	DG V
	Ralf Jacob	DG V
	Ana Melich	DG X
	Roger O'Keeffe	DG XXII
	Stefaan de Rynck	DG XVI
	Marjorie Jouen (co-ord.)	Forward Studies Unit
	Gilles Bertrand	Forward Studies Unit
Group 3: Economic adaptability	Michel Biart	DG V
	Paraskevas Caracostas	DG XII
	Pierre Deusy-Fournier	DG VIII

David Hudson	DG I
Fabienne Ilzkowitz	DG II
Carlos Martinez Mongay	DG II
Adriaan Dierx	DG II
Willem Noë	DG III
John Norman Pyres	DG XXII
Denis Redonnet	DG II
Alain Stekke	DG XIII
Renate Weissenhorn	DG XXIII
Francis Woehrling	DG II
Lucio R. Pench (co-ord.)	Forward Studies Unit
Gilles Bertrand	Forward Studies Unit

Group 4: Enlargement	Jean-Louis de Brouwer	Task Force Justice & 　Home Affairs
	Fraser Cameron	DG IA
	Jean-François Drevet	DG XVI
	David Hudson	DG I
	Lotte Knudsen	DG IA
	Christian Leffler	Secretariat General
	Colin Imrie	Task Force Justice & 　Home Affairs
	Willem Noë	DG III
	Joan Pearce	DG II
	Philippe Renaudière	DG XV
	Axel Walldén	DG IA
	Sabine Weyand	DG I
	Anna Michalski (co-ord.)	Forward Studies Unit
	Gilles Bertrand	Forward Studies Unit

Group 5: International environment	Véronique Arnault	DG I
	Fraser Cameron	DG IA
	Roy Dickinson	DG I
	Michael Green	DG IB
	Sean Greenaway	ECHO
	Marcel Leroy	DG VIII
	Peter Meyer	DG IA
	Anna Michalski	Forward Studies Unit
	Andrea Mogni	DG IB
	Joan Pearce	DG II
	Agne Pantelouri (co-ord.)	Forward Studies Unit
	Gilles Bertrand	Forward Studies Unit

Steering group	Michel Biart	DG V
(synthesis and	Paraskevas Caracostas	DG XII
production of the	Jean-François Drevet	DG XVI
global scenarios)	David Hudson	DG I
	Ana Melich	DG X
	John Norman Pyres	DG XXII
	Adrian Taylor	DG IB
	Axel Walldén	DG IA
	Francis Woehrling	DG II
	Gilles Bertrand (co-ord.)	Forward Studies Unit
	Anna Michalski (co-ord.)	Forward Studies Unit
	Lucio R. Pench (co-ord.)	Forward Studies Unit

Directorates-General quoted in the list:

DG I	External relations: Commercial policy and relations with North America, the Far East, Australia and New Zealand
DG IA	External relations: Europe and the New Independent States, Common Foreign and Security Policy and External Missions
DG IB	External relations: Southern Mediterranean, Middle and Near East, Latin America, South and South East Asia and North–South Co-operation
DG II	Economic and Financial Affairs
DG III	Industry
DG V	Employment, Industrial Relations and Social Affairs
DG VIII	Development
DG IX	Personnel and Administration
DG X	Information, Communication, Culture, Audio-visual
DG XII	Science, Research and Development
DG XIII	Telecommunications, Information Market and Exploitation of Research
DG XV	Internal Market and Financial Services
DG XVI	Regional policies and Cohesion
DG XIX	Budgets
DG XXII	Education, Training and Youth
DG XXIII	Enterprise Policy, Distributive Trades, Tourism and Co-operatives
ECHO	European Community Humanitarian Office

Index